EMMA BUNTON

Mama You Got This

A LITTLE HELPING HAND
FOR NEW PARENTS

EBURY
PRESS

Me and mummy Bunton

CONTENTS

Hi there Mama!

Most of you know me for being a Spice Girl, but the achievement I am proudest of in my life is being a mum to my two children. This book is a celebration of your brilliantness for making and having your child. Wow!

Isn't that amazing? Yes, but it's also pretty terrifying, and probably why so many of us reach for a book, just like you are doing right now, hoping it will tell us what to do and take some of this giant responsibility off our hands. If I've learnt one thing about loving and caring for your own child, it's that no one has the definitive guide. All of us are on our own paths, and you are quite literally the only expert in the field of you and your baby.

If you are looking for a how-to instruction manual, this book isn't going to help you. I won't pretend I haven't tried plenty of them – I bought every book on the shelf when my babies were born, but they all seemed to be too prescriptive.

My two babies

It was all sleep regimes and feeding schedules and rules for being a green parent or a free-range parent, or whatever kind of parent was happening that week. I was interested in all of those things, but I also didn't need something else on my to-do list. I had enough on my plate as it was, without feeling like I was supposed to be doing even more things, and getting those wrong too!

What I really, really wanted was a book I could reach for in the middle of the night, when I was so tired I could hardly open my eyes and the milk was pouring out of my boobs and the baby was having a big cry. A book that would give me the information and support I needed without judgement, without making me feel like a failure. A book that would give me honest advice, and might even make me chuckle occasionally. Basically, I needed a book that was also my best mate. But not in a fluffy or patronising way. I needed the kind of best mate who gives it to you straight, when your hair looks rubbish or your outfit isn't working.

Because even though I had all the real-life girl power of the actual Spice Girls on speed-dial, as well as my incredible partner Jade and my tireless mum Pauline, I still needed that extra reassurance, something to check in with, to make sure I was getting it right. Sometimes it felt a bit like even those nearest and dearest to me didn't always want to tell me the truth. Why had no one told me, for example, that breastfeeding could be painful or that I would still look pregnant two months after I'd given birth? Why did no one tell me?! That was the question I asked most in those first few months and years, not always out loud.

I've since realised that a lot of fibbing goes on in this motherhood game! I reckon it's a survival strategy. Us women shield each other from the realities of childbirth and having babies, because, let's be honest, if we knew the half of it, we might not sign up for the job so willingly. And then where would the human race be?

Other times, people do tell you things about motherhood, but you don't really get what they mean. Or maybe you just don't want to hear it. People tell you that babies keep you up at night and you're going to feel tired, but you don't really understand quite how exhausted a new baby can make you feel, until you are living it. People tell you you'll love your baby like you've never loved anyone before, but you don't really get it until they are in your arms looking at you like a genuine angel from heaven.

By the time Beau arrived in 2007, I'd been a Spice Girl for over a decade. Some of the big worries new mums have today hadn't even been imagined yet: climate change still only happened in far-off lands and few people knew what a dairy intolerance was; even being a working mother was still kind of a novelty. Nonetheless, I felt I knew a thing or two about challenge. I'd spent most of my twenties living life on what you might call a gruelling schedule: daily rehearsals and physical training, late night performances and long-haul flights (while also having the absolute time of my life with four of my best friends). I'd performed in front of millions of people all over the world, met the Queen at Buckingham Palace and had tea at Nelson Mandela's house. I could deal with a baby, no problem.

Ha! Nothing could have prepared me. It wasn't just the sheer physical challenge of it all, but the knowing that I was responsible for this little bundle I had just made, and loved so unexpectedly fiercely. Despite all my experience overcoming nerves on stage and being in the spotlight, I surprised myself by being quite an anxious new mum.

I look back now and laugh at how I panicked over the littlest things. Like the time I noticed Beau had little red spots all over his face and phoned my health visitor, convinced he'd contracted some kind of terrible plague. 'They're milk spots,' she said calmly, 'totally normal. Try squirting some breast milk on them and they should go away.' You want me to squirt milk from my boobs at my new baby's face? Are you sure? But true enough, they calmed down with a little smidge of milk! Every day it seemed like something else unexpected would happen and send me into panic mode. When Tate came along four years later, I assumed I would feel more in control. I was a pro this time, right? But it turns out that a second new baby is a whole new riddle to figure out, when you haven't even solved the first one yet. I'd been a woman feeling at the top of my game for years, and yet here I was, quite often feeling like a nervous wreck. Where was the book that would tell me what I needed to know, without either glossing over the details or giving me a list of impossible rules to follow?

It's here! I wrote it for you, so you don't have to feel the same frustration when no one has told you that baby poo looks weird when they eat bananas or that changing bags are an entirely optional purchase. I'm sharing my stories and experiences with you, so we can have a laugh and a cry together along the way. I'm here in this book whenever you need me, night or day.

I've never written a book before, so if you're wondering why I've chosen this moment in time to share my story, let me give you some background.

In 2017 I launched the eco-friendly nappy range Kit & Kin. I've learnt so much from creating it that I want to share. Why did I launch a nappy range? When I was a new mum there were two big issues that really challenged me; starting Kit & Kin was

Before and after our world changed

my way of trying to answer the questions I had back then, and helping others who might not have the answers now.

Issue number 1

Eczema and skin irritation were big problems for both of my babies, especially Tate. As a family we spent a lot of time going back and forth to doctors about their skin, trying every cream and emollient out there, but everything seemed to treat the symptoms and not the cause. We didn't realise back then that regular disposable nappies and wipes contain chemicals and unnecessary skin irritants. It wasn't until much later on that I learnt that there were more natural alternatives that could do the same job and reduce the impact on babies' skin.

Issue number 2

The mountain of disposable nappies sitting in landfill somewhere with my family's name on it weighed heavily on my mind. I felt so guilty! But those first few months were such an incredibly busy time, I didn't really have the headspace to think about it. And back then there weren't any more planet-friendly alternatives to turn to. The only other option was towelling nappies, and they weren't easy to use in those days at all (more on washables including Kit & Kin's game-changing range on page 144). It was easier, necessary even, to put that guilt out of my mind and just try to get through the days with everyone in one piece.

Creating Kit & Kin was a way for me to address both of these experiences in a positive way that might help other parents and make their lives easier. I'm unbelievably proud to have developed these nappies, along with the all-natural skincare range and now our organic cotton babywear. It's up there with being a Spice Girl as one of the best things I've ever done (having my children has the number one spot, obviously!). And even though my kids are well out of nappies now, the memories of when they were in them seem like yesterday (there's loads more on nappies and all things baby wee and poop in Chapter 4). Writing this book is a way to share all my memories, all the highs and lows, all that I've learnt, and keep on making that difference.

I've also pulled in help and guidance from some of the best experts in the game. Because being a mama was so all-consuming and so completely new to me, I always loved it when people gave me advice. It didn't matter whether it was medical advice from a doctor, an old wives' tale from my mum's hairdresser (I got a few tips from her; loved them!) or the wise words of a weary soundman when we were on tour. I had a big appetite for all the incredible knowledge those who had been there before me had to offer.

And that's what I wanted to do here with *Mama You Got This*. From the sleep expert beloved of my US friends to the British midwife specialising in neonatal skin, the people I've gathered together to help you are people who I have worked with, or who have been recommended to me by friends and family, who I know have the kind of experience we all want when it comes to our babies (and ourselves). There are so many amazing experts out there today, and ways of doing things now, that are so brilliant. I wish I'd had the information I have now, back then. So I've gathered some of the best of it to share with you in this book alongside my own stories.

I've also asked these guys to contribute and share, because it gives you a range of tried-and-tested options to consider, rather than one fix-all solution that makes you feel bad if it doesn't work for you. A whole team of amazing world-class experts are right here, on hand to help you out!

But don't worry, you won't find feeding schedules or judgey rants about co-sleeping or whether baby-wearing is a thing – I know I didn't find any of that stuff helpful and I'm no good with rules at all. Parenting theories and routines for this or that are not what this is about. What I hope my book will do is give you clear, balanced information and honest, no-frills advice on only the stuff that matters, to help you make the decisions that are right for you.

I've kept the focus on the first 12 months, simply because it was such an extraordinary time, both times around… bringing my babies home for the first time, figuring out how to feed them, adjusting to the new me who was now also a mum, as well as things like friendships, relationships and, of course, being a Spice Girl. Chapters cover off all the big themes like feeding, sleeping, playing with your baby, weaning and looking after yourself, so you can quickly find the information you need when you don't have time to sit down with a cuppa and read from start to finish.

I want this book to give you the confidence and the inner strength to feel good about being a new mum, to trust your instincts, even – or maybe especially – if your instinct is to ask for help. I want it to be that friend, the one who tells it to you straight, maybe sometimes a bit too straight, but who you know you can trust. Because the more we can all reach out and help each other, the better we are all going to feel about this amazing experience called motherhood.

I want you to feel like you've got this, because guess what, mama? You have!

love, Emma x

Beau on tour with us

Meet Team Mama

Let me introduce you to the team of incredible experts I have called in to help me help you in this book:

CHRISTOPHER MONEY
kitandkin.com

Chris is the co-founder of Kit & Kin, he's a dad, and he has over 15 years' experience developing and manufacturing sustainable products for mothers and babies that are better for our planet, and that give back.

JULIA MINCHIN
@hippychickbaby

Julia Minchin is a mother of three and the designer of an award-winning baby carrier. She knows a thing or two about slings and carriers and has some great tips to share about choosing the right one for you and your baby.

HEIDI FULTON
heidifulton.com

California-based Heidi is a mindfulness and emotional resolution coach and mum of three. She teaches mindfulness in schools and works with new mums to help them find peace and balance.

FRAN BAILEY
@nct

Fran is an experienced NCT breastfeeding counsellor and specialist feeding practitioner, who has been delivering antenatal and postnatal education to new parents for almost 20 years. She also helped the charity set up a postnatal drop-in for refugee and asylum-seeking women.

DIANA SPALDING
@mother.ly

US-based midwife Diana Spalding, MSN, CNM is a certified nurse-midwife, paediatric nurse and mother of three. She's also the Health and Wellness Director at Motherly and author of the excellent *Motherly Guide to Becoming Mama: Redefining the Pregnancy, Birth and Postpartum Journey*.

DR CRAIG CANAPARI

@drcanapari

Dr Craig Canapari is a paediatric sleep consultant at Yale University and a father of two. He's also the author of *It's Never Too Late to Sleep Train: The Low-Stress Way to High-Quality Sleep for Babies, Kids and Parents* and writes regularly for the *New York Times* on the subject of infant sleep.

MARLEY HALL

@midwifemarley

Marley Hall has been a midwife for over a decade. She's safely delivered thousands of new babies into the world and held the hands of their amazing mamas all the way through birth and beyond. She's also a pretty amazing mama herself, with five of her own children to prove it!

MARIE LOUISE

@the_modern_midwife

Marie Louise, aka The Modern Midwife, is a mum of one and an NHS midwife with over a decade's experience helping new mums and their babies. She's the author of *The Modern Midwife's Guide to Pregnancy, Birth & Beyond* and has a special interest in neonatal skin.

DR SAM WASS

@uelbabydevlab/@drsamwass

Dr Sam Wass is a child psychologist and father of two. You might recognise him from Channel 4's *The Secret Life of…* series, but he's also the neuroscientist heading up the BabyDevLab at the University of East London.

BECCY HANDS & ALEXIS STICKLAND

@the_mother_box

Doula Beccy Hands and midwife Alexis Stickland, from The Mother Box, specialise in looking after new mums and have lots of great advice to share about the very important art of self-care.

ALEXIS RALPHS

@onehundredtoys

Alexis Ralphs is a father of four. He was an early years teacher for 13 years before he founded One Hundred Toys, a company specialising in learning through play for babies and the under-fives whose ethos is 'fewer, better toys'.

You Made a Baby! Now What?

SETTLING INTO NEW LIFE AS A MAMA

Chapter One

It was August and I remember
it was muggy, but I couldn't
tell you much else about the
journey home that day...

I don't remember leaving the hospital or putting the car seat
in; I don't remember what I was wearing or what my bag was
like; I don't remember what route we took home or anything
much about it at all. The only thing I do remember is sitting
in the back, as close as I possibly could to the car seat, and
just staring at Beau as we shifted quietly through the busy
London traffic.

His tiny fingers with their perfect miniature nails were
clamped so strongly around my index finger all the way home,
and I just couldn't stop staring at my baby! Here was the most
incredible, beautiful thing I'd ever seen, and I couldn't believe
I was his mama.

I'd spent three nights in the hospital. That hadn't been part of the plan, but I was two weeks overdue so the natural birth I'd imagined had gone up the spout, and I'd ended up having a caesarean section. (I am forever grateful I didn't make one of those really detailed birth plans, because I know I'd have been really disappointed that things hadn't gone as they were supposed to!). The midwives and the nurses on the ward had all been so wonderful and had looked after us so well. I'd had a reaction to the anaesthetic at one point, and was throwing up and itching all over; after that I was sobbing, overwhelmed with all this love I had for my baby, my hormones crashing about all over the place. Being around these wise, calm women, who reassured me that everything I was going through was 100 per cent normal, was exactly what I needed in those first few days. I think I would happily have stayed another three days, and possibly three more after that.

But even though I'd enjoyed the cocoon and reassurance of the hospital, nothing could ever have felt as special as coming home. My partner Jade and I had been trying for a baby for what had, by then, been a long time. We'd been living in what we thought of as our family home, saving a space for this little person to join our life. Bringing him through that door was like finding the final piece of a very big jigsaw (although I didn't know yet that there was still another piece to find: Tate, who would come along four years later).

That was a special moment – when the front door closed behind us with its familiar sound and there we were, the three of us, home at last. We sat ourselves down on the sofa and just stared at Beau again as he slept, his little mouth moving from time to time as he dozed. Here he was then, my son, a vision of bliss in the little white onesie and soft cotton hat with the bear ears on. We took in every feature, working out from whose gene pool his face shape and his hair and his ears all came from. I hadn't anticipated just how fascinating my baby would be. I felt like I could sit and marvel at him forever. I'm not sure I've ever stopped.

That peace didn't last long though; visitors started to arrive. We've always been a sociable family and love having a house full of fun and laughter, so I had always imagined being so eager to share the love and introduce everyone to my baby. And don't get me wrong, I definitely did want to show him off – I was so proud of him! But I was also surprised by the sense of unease that I felt if he got passed around too much by well-meaning friends who wanted cuddles. I found myself watching people holding him, checking they had his head supported properly, or wondering if they had too much perfume on. I kept taking him back off people if I felt they had held him for too long. I was feeling all these animal instincts and emotions, primal urges to protect and nurture, that I hadn't really felt before. Mama Bear had arrived!

I also found myself going into hygiene overdrive. I don't know where it came from, but I needed to make sure everything was clean. Even though I was breastfeeding, I had a steriliser set up and made sure all his dummies and toys, and pretty much everything that he came into contact with, were sterilised (see the next chapter on page 49 for more on feeding). And I asked everyone to wash their hands when they came in the house and before they held him. In fact, I bought so much hand sanitiser that when the COVID-19 pandemic struck in 2020 I still had drawers full of the stuff. (I laugh at myself, but I know that for some people the urge to clean can become problematic and may be a way of coping with postnatal anxiety. If you think this might be the case, talk to your health visitor or GP. It's not as uncommon as you might think and there is lots of help out there, from cognitive behavioural therapy (CBT) to counselling.)

In those first few days and weeks, as people popped round with all their lovely gifts and good wishes, I realised that the world was now made up of two groups of people: those who got it and those who didn't. The people who got it were the ones who turned up with a home-made shepherd's pie or baked me a big cake, because they knew I was ravenously hungry now I was breastfeeding. They were the ones who made a cuppa or brought me a glass of water while I fed the baby and didn't expect me to look after them. They were the people who rolled up their sleeves and didn't behave like guests at all. They left after an hour or so, because they knew that was about all we could cope with. I'll always remember the one friend who unloaded my dishwasher – a simple act of kindness that at that moment seemed like the loveliest thing anyone had ever done for me. Because when you have a new baby at home, what you really want when someone comes over is not to chat to them, it's some help.

Even though they are mostly asleep and can't yet move or talk or do anything much, new babies are experts at taking up extraordinary amounts of your time. Don't ask me how, but some days in those first few weeks, I couldn't even find five minutes to get properly dressed. Finishing a whole cup of tea felt like a real achievement. Hours and hours seemed to vanish as I moved from feed to sleep to change to feed again. And when I wasn't doing any of that, I could easily lose another few hours just being fascinated by my baby and every tiny little thing he did.

So when those visitors who didn't get it came round, it felt kind of stressful. I remember when we'd only been home a couple of days, some really good friends came over with a couple of bottles of champagne. It was lovely to see them and share a glass to celebrate (even if mine was sparkling water!), but when that was over, they didn't make the noises about leaving I was listening out for, and instead cracked open another bottle. Before Beau, I'd have been well up for sipping champers with these guys, but now all I could think about was how I was going to get them to leave so that I could put him down for a nap and try to get some sleep in myself. They were showing no signs of going and in the end I had to text my mum on the sly to get her to come round and pretend she wanted some time with me! As we finally waved them off about four hours later, the penny dropped: my life would never be the same again. My priorities had changed. Everything had changed.

I also realised that I had been that very person! The one who held the baby just slightly too long and stayed for that second glass of wine when I probably should have left them to it. I had been someone who didn't get it. How would you know, until it happens to you? So when Tate came along, I was much better prepared and felt more able to say no if people suggested popping round at a difficult time or if I was invited to something I just knew I couldn't cope with. Although that wasn't always easy, either. I know I upset a good friend by not going to her thirtieth birthday party (the thought of a late night filled me with dread), and another whose child-free wedding I had to say no to (she thought I could just get a babysitter and leave them!). And of course Beau was around this time, so guests and visitors became welcome distractions for the older child, while I looked after Tate. Many a guest who had come to see Tate was dolefully dispatched to the park with Beau for an hour instead! In fact, far from being jealous of a new sibling (as people had warned me might happen), I think Beau enjoyed all the extra attention he got.

My coming home essentials

You're going to be spending a lot of time at home with your new baby. Stock up on all the essentials, so you can relax and not have to be rushing out to buy things. Here are my top tips for the things you'll need:

- **Breast pads.**
- **Maternity pads.**
- **Big black knickers and a few decent maternity bras.** Go for cotton where you can, as it is breathable, regulates your temperature and lets any broken skin heal naturally.
- **Soft, comfy clothes like joggers** that are easy to pull on and off (with no zips or buckles) and big, loose tops that are easy to lift up for feeding, and that hide all the lumps and bumps.
- **All your favourite body lotions, gels and oils** (just keep them natural and unscented so you don't risk aggravating your baby's skin).

- **Flannels.** Sometimes a stand-up wash is all you can manage, especially if you have scars in delicate places.
- **Home-cooked meals in the freezer** for easy dinner times and lots of healthy snacks in the cupboard.
- **A spoonful of Manuka honey for mum.** Nature's antibiotic!
- **Dry shampoo.** There is never a better time to cheat on your hair regime.
- **Nipple cream.** It can take a while for your nipples to adjust so have some lanolin-based cream at the ready (see Chapter Two, page 72 for more on this).
- **Exercise ball.** Comfy for you and baby, and gives your glutes a little workout too.

Lotions and potions

I loved all my gels and creams and lotions and potions during those first few weeks. I've always been a sucker for a nice body lotion or a good hand cream. Jade has always moisturised every day as well, so it had always been a part of our routine at home anyway. I really found sanctuary in them during pregnancy and afterwards. When you are spending so much time at home trying to heal, and giving so much of yourself to a tiny little person, taking just a few minutes to moisturise and nourish your skin can feel like a mini spa break. I moisturised my bump with cocoa butter all through my first pregnancy as I'd been worried about stretch marks (it didn't work – I got them anyway! I think everyone does. I'm quite fond of them now) and, once I'd given birth, I got myself a whole cabinet full of gels and balms for places on my body I'd never even considered before. I had belly butter and perineum balm, nipple gel, boob cream and scrubs for everything – there was not a part of my body that I didn't moisturise or protect with some kind of oil or gel or both during that early period of being at home. It was a small gesture of self-care at a time when I could barely get to brush my hair (I also got through a lot of dry shampoo I seem to remember!).

Someone gave me a big, soft, cotton shawl with sleeves that I wrapped around myself every day. It was so warm and cocooning, like my own grown-up swaddling blanket. I never took it off. I don't think there is one photo from that period where I'm not wearing that shawl! I used to put it on and sit on my exercise ball and gently bounce with the baby in my arms – I must have looked mad now I think about it! But I didn't care. Both babies really responded well to it (usually by going to sleep) because I guess for them it felt like being in the womb, and for me it was a way of sitting down that took the pressure off my aching hips and pelvis, as they recovered from the strain of pregnancy.

Me, Beau, and my shawl!

Try some scar massage

—

If you've had a C-section or an episiotomy, or have torn naturally and needed stitches, then chances are you'll have a scar or two to show for it. For the first six weeks, scars can feel a bit itchy and uncomfortable as your body works its magic and heals the skin. During this stage it's best to simply keep your scar clean, washing it with warm water and a clean flannel – you don't need to put anything on it, apart from perhaps a little fresh air to help it along. Once you've had your postnatal check (usually at six weeks) and as long as there is no open skin or scabs, you can do a little massage to help reduce the scar tissue either on your perineum or your tummy. Use an organic, natural oil, like coconut or almond (nothing scented), and gently massage the scar area with your fingertips, applying pressure and moving in circles over the scar. Do this for a few minutes, two or three times a day, and you should eventually reduce any bumps or tenderness left by your scar.

Just Be

While I loved this early time at home, I also had this nagging sense that I should somehow be getting back to 'normal' more quickly. The body positivity movement hadn't yet been thought of; I love how women are so much more honest about their bodies today, and are sharing realistic images of themselves online and on social media. But back then it seemed like every day there was another story in the press about a celebrity mum who had miraculously returned to her 'pre-baby body' or who had lost her 'baby weight' in record time.

Having a C-section scar means you can't go around lifting weights and doing spin classes anyway. It was way more delicate than I had imagined it would be (how did they get a whole baby out of there?) and there were still what looked suspiciously like office staples in my stomach, while it healed. With the bruises and the wobbly flesh and the bleeding scar, I genuinely looked and felt like Frankenstein in those first few weeks. But even if I hadn't had the scars, there was no way I could imagine hitting a hardcore exercise regime so soon after I'd had my children. I was morbidly fascinated by the stories about the training and the diets and the surgery that some women were putting themselves through, so they could look like they hadn't just given birth. I just wanted to be wrapped up in my shawl and my comfy clothes with my pillows, cuddling my baby!

Even so, I did try to get back to 'normal' too soon. When Beau was just three months old, I found myself on an aeroplane heading to LA for a Spice Girls reunion tour. I don't mind admitting now, with the benefit of hindsight, that this was too early to be getting back on stage. I was lucky that I could take Beau with me to work, and feed him and see him when I wasn't performing. And, of course, Jade and Mum were around to help. But being one fifth of the Spice Girls requires major physical stamina; daily rehearsals, long journeys, late nights in unfamiliar beds. When Beau went to bed at 7pm each night, I didn't go and have a nice relaxing bath and get an early night, I went on stage and performed in front of hundreds of thousands of people in huge arenas.

They say the body keeps the score, and my body certainly let me know it wasn't ready for this. I kept falling over backstage, I cried at everything, my skin broke out in rashes. When I asked our physio what he thought was wrong with me, he just looked at me and laughed, 'There's nothing wrong with you! You've just had a baby; your body is still recovering.'

This was my first glimpse of the juggling act we mothers have to learn, between nurturing the career you have spent a lifetime building and the new life you have just created. Us mums are always juggling. You've got to keep those balls in the air mama! But don't worry, you are going to drop quite a few, and that's OK!

With Tate I felt less pressure to instantly become this superwoman juggling supremo, and knew better than to make any plans for a while. I kept my to-do lists shorter, so when the evening came round and I hadn't even managed to find a stamp, let alone post a thank you card, I didn't feel like such a failure.

But certainly with your first, it takes a while for the new you and the old you to make their peace with one another. As women we are all under so much pressure to achieve time, to be brilliant at everything, including being a mum.

Like I said, us mamas are always juggling!

Sometimes we have to take our foot off the pedal and just accept that we're going to be at home for a bit, ideally in a shawl with some biscuits close by. I found adjusting to this easier than I expected, but I know sometimes it can be really hard for new mums.

Us mums are always juggling. You've got to keep those balls in the air mama! But don't worry, you are going to drop quite a few and that's OK!

Top tip

—

If you don't already practise mindfulness and think it's not for you, don't be put off by the name! There is no yoga or 'omming' required. You don't have to be all spiritual to use this technique and it might just help you focus on the important stuff: you and your baby.

Have you tried mindfulness meditation?

—

My mum Pauline practises reiki and reflexology, so I grew up around healing therapies and self-care concepts that were probably considered to be kind of alternative back then (there's lots more on this, including some tips from my mum, in Chapter Six, page 209). And yet, even though these ideas were familiar to me (or maybe because they were so familiar!), I still struggled to find the peace I needed sometimes, when I felt like I had a hundred things to do and couldn't get past the first. Mindfulness meditation has become more mainstream now and is a great way to recentre and ground yourself when everything feels a bit crazy.

There are lots of mindfulness apps and books out there, but here are a couple of simple exercises from California-based mindfulness coach Heidi Fulton to try right now:

TAKE IT FROM THE EXPERT

HEIDI FULTON – MINDFULNESS COACH

❝ Feeling calm and steady is what most of us want for ourselves and our babies, but it's not always possible, especially when we are feeling tired or sad or overwhelmed. Our babies are constantly attuning to our moods and feelings. That's why it's important to really focus on being with them, to let them know we are here and that everything is OK.

Try this when your baby is feeding. As tempting as it is to check your Instagram feed, instead try being completely present with your baby and take in the experience using all your senses.

Take in their expressions, their smell,
the soft eyelids, twitching nose, the little
mouth sucking away.

Absorb the suckling sounds and the soft weight
of them in your arms; the tugging and the
little hands clutching at the breast or bottle.
Absorb and savour all of these sensations, and
notice how they make you feel inside.

You can also do this when you're giving
them a bath, cuddling them before bedtime
or just having a quiet few moments with
them lying on your chest. Your baby will
feel your presence and your attention in
that moment, helping to regulate both
yours and your baby's nervous systems.

To help yourself deal with negative emotions
and feelings, take a moment to tune in
to that difficult emotion. This may sound
counter-intuitive, but it's a proven practice
and actually very healing. Whether you're
tired or tetchy or feeling low, notice what
it feels like in your body.

Sit down, close your eyes and feel the
physical sensations of that emotion inside
your body. Every emotion is made up of a
series of physical sensations. Maybe you feel
frustration as a tightness in your chest, a

swirling in your stomach or a constricted throat. By watching and feeling the changing, moving sensations in your body, you're no longer reacting to them. Instead you are metabolising them, digesting them. The more we suppress emotions, the bigger they become. When we allow ourselves to feel them, they simply pass through us and make space for something else. Maybe peace or even joy.

,

Another thing I've learnt about since my time at home with newborns is what midwives and doulas call the 'fourth trimester'. As the name suggests, the idea is that pregnancy, in fact, has an additional fourth stage that takes place once the baby has been born. Experts believe that, in this period, both mama and baby need rest and quiet time to heal and recover from the huge physical process that is birth, and for baby to acclimatise to life outside the womb. I wish I'd known about the fourth trimester! I think so many of us feel it intuitively, but identifying this early period as a gentle time for mama and baby gives us the permission we need to really focus on our recovery and getting to know our babies.

Check out what superwoman midwife Marley Hall has to say about the fourth trimester in the next pages. In the meantime, my message to you is this: don't be afraid to stop and allow yourself to enjoy this special time at home with your baby. It's OK to say no to things for a bit, the visitors can come another time. Don't worry about decorating the spare room or trying to lose weight. Curl up and rest up for now, mama. You're going to need your strength!

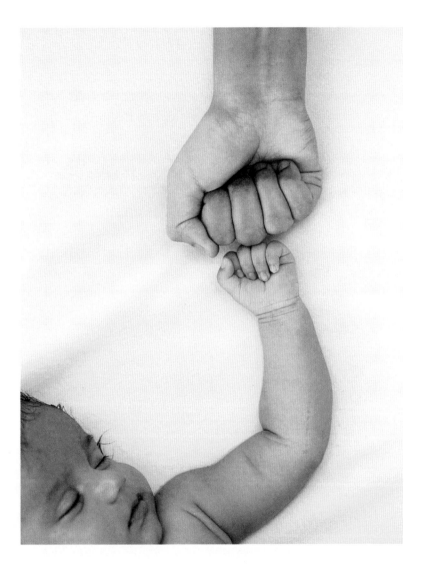

You Made a Baby! Now What?

One thing you really don't need

—

A puppy! Jade thought it would be a great idea to buy me a chocolate Labrador puppy just before we had Beau. What was he thinking? I know his intentions were good, but frankly it was the last thing I needed! We muddled through (in fact we even bought another one, Jojo, to keep Phoebe company), but at times I thought I'd lost my mind, it was such chaos. Especially when they ripped apart my new sofas. Like, actually ripped them to pieces! It turned out that Phoebe was the best big sister a baby could ask for, and was so loving and protective of Beau. She'd sit by him night and day. But if you can avoid inviting the carnage that is a new puppy into your home while you have a young baby, I'd recommend putting it off until a little later.

Curl up and rest up for now, mama. You're going to need your strength!

The Fourth Trimester

Midwife Marley Hall knows a thing or two about babies: she's got five of her own for starters! But she's also been a midwife for over ten years and has looked after thousands of newborns and their amazing mamas. Here she answers all your questions about the fourth trimester and why you need it in your life:

TAKE IT FROM THE EXPERT

MARLEY HALL – MIDWIFE

THE FOURTH TRIMESTER

❝ The fourth trimester describes the 12-week period following the birth of your baby. It's not a medical term, but it has gained recognition in recent years as a way to help parents get to grips with the normal needs and behaviours of their babies in the early days. Looking at the fourth trimester as an accepted stage in the process of having your baby can help to reduce the worry and stress that often comes with newborns; things like wondering why your baby is crying so much, why they want to be held all the time or why they don't sleep through the night like adults. I've found that parents who are on board with the idea of a fourth trimester can often find the shock of a newborn baby less difficult to cope with.

WHAT DOES THE FOURTH TRIMESTER MEAN FOR MY BABY?

After spending nine months in the womb, not having to worry about food, temperature or security, suddenly your baby is propelled into a world of noise, bright lights and varying temperatures. Their never-ending supply of food has stopped and they need to work to maintain their own body temperature, which is difficult for newborns. This is some pretty big stuff for a baby! It's a time of major adjustment, and survival. They want to be close to their food source — you. And it's normal for them to cry when you put them down ('Don't leave me!') and settle down when you pick them up ('Phew, you're here'). As difficult as it can be for a parent to actually get anything done, babies are designed this way!

You cannot 'spoil' them by responding to their cries. Crying is the only way they can communicate with you and responding to their cries is the right thing to do.

TOP TIP

If your baby cries a lot at first, try wearing them in a sling. This means they're happy because they're close to you (their food source) and you can get on with a few jobs, if you have the energy. It can be a tricky time, but remember it's not forever. They grow so fast and, before you know it, they're crawling around touching everything within sight! (For more on slings and carriers, head to Chapter Five, page 183.)

WHAT DOES THE FOURTH TRIMESTER MEAN FOR ME?

The fourth trimester for mums is what we call the postnatal or postpartum stage. There are lots of physical and emotional changes that can happen during this time.

'This should be a time when you are getting to know your baby, learning to feed them and also simply resting. Don't be afraid to ask friends and family for help and support — it's important that you are looked after too.'

—

MARLEY HALL

Physical healing

If you have perineal or C-section wounds
and most of us do), they will be sore.
Postpartum bleeding (from your vagina) can
go on for several weeks, as the placental
site starts to heal over. You may also
experience 'afterpains'where the uterus
continues to contract after the birth to
reduce its size. This is more common with
second and subsequent births and it may
be more noticeable during feeds if you
are breastfeeding.

Emotional changes

Having a baby can be overwhelming. The birth,
lack of sleep and the new responsibility of
having a newborn can really take their toll
on you emotionally. Knowing what to expect can
help to bolster your emotions around this time.

Don't focus on entertaining guests or things
that can be sorted out later — now is not
the time to start building an extension.
This should be a time when you are getting
to know your baby, learning to feed them and
also simply resting. Don't be afraid to ask
friends and family for help and support —
it's important that you are looked after too.

A shift in hormones after the birth often exacerbates feelings of low mood. Somewhere around day three or four, you may experience what is called the 'three-day blues' when you feel a bit tearful. This is really common and affects up to 85 per cent of new mums. If you continue to feel low over the coming weeks, speak to a health professional, such as a GP, midwife or health visitor, as it may be postnatal depression. Postnatal depression is common, and again understanding, and not underestimating the fourth trimester can really help you to cope. (See Chapter Six, page 207 for more on coping with low mood.)

Fatigue

Babies often cry a lot during the fourth trimester. They may suffer with colic (continuous crying for at least three hours a day — sometimes due to abdominal pain or wind), which can also be distressing. Babies feed often, and for the first couple of months they are unlikely to go for longer than five hours during the night without being fed. This can be exhausting. Know that it is normal for babies to do this and that they will sleep a little longer in their own time.

Cluster feeding is another normal but tiring time, especially if you are breastfeeding (bottle-fed babies cluster feed too and this is tiring in its own way!). <u>Cluster feeding is when your baby feeds more than usual, because they're going through a growth spurt.</u> Sometimes they go as little as 20 minutes between feeds for a certain portion of the day. This can go on for a few days at a time, feeding frequently to encourage the breast to produce more milk. This is exactly as draining as it sounds, but is usually short-lived. You can expect to experience this several times in the fourth trimester.

WHAT SHOULD I DO TO PREPARE FOR THE FOURTH TRIMESTER?

Try to remove all your expectations about how it's going to be. You just can't know how you will feel as you recover from birth, what a baby's temperament will be like or how you'll feel about everything.

If you buy (or borrow) one thing, a sling lets you 'wear' your baby while also having your hands free so you can do things like eating and drinking. It's a winner!

TOP TIP

Make up a spot on the sofa with a basket
full of everything you need in easy
reach: healthy snacks, water bottle,
nappies, phone charger, book. You will
be spending a lot of your time there,
so be prepared!

Remember, there is no textbook that will
tell you how your baby will behave. Go with
the flow, learn from your baby and trust your
instincts. If you have any concerns, get in
touch with your GP, midwife or health visitor.

'

You Made a Baby! Now What?

Boobs, Bottles and Beyond!

ON BECOMING A HUMAN MILK FLOAT

Chapter Two

I'm Booby Spice! We came up with this new name for me in the hospital, when I was feeding Beau for one of the very first times and my boobs had ballooned to epic proportions with the milk coming in.

I tried not to laugh too hard, as I didn't want to disturb Beau during what seemed to be going pretty well, for two absolute beginners like me and him. From that moment on, I was Booby Spice.

I'd known from early on that I wanted to at least try breastfeeding. I'm lucky to have a liberal circle of friends: some have never breastfed at all and others have done it for years, but there was never any pressure or judgement from the people around me to choose breast- over bottle-feeding. But I know that pressure exists, and that it is a very specific kind of quiet and judgemental pressure, one that only women seem to put on each other.

Are you under bressure?

—

In 2015 a survey from Channel Mum found that 69 per cent of mums who fed their babies with a bottle had received cruel or negative comments from other mums for not breastfeeding, and 40 per cent who bottle-fed said they felt like they had failed their child. There was even a Twitter hashtag about the pressure to breastfeed: #bressure.

I know that for some new mums there is a real sense of disappointment and sadness if breastfeeding doesn't work out. I even know of one mum who felt so embarrassed that she couldn't get on with breastfeeding that she lied to her health visitor and told her she was doing it anyway! I managed not to carry any of that expectation around with me. I knew I wanted to give it a go, and of course I wondered if I would be able to do it, but I was also prepared to switch to the bottle without giving myself too much of a hard time, if that was what I needed to do. After all, I wasn't breastfed, and I didn't turn out too bad, did I?

But I definitely wanted to try. The health benefits of breastfeeding are undeniable (see what Fran Bailey has to say over on page 64) and the World Health Organization (WHO) recommends it for the first six months of life.

I really wanted to give breastfeeding a go but I wasn't breastfed, and I didn't turn out too bad, did I?

The official line on breastfeeding

—

The WHO and UNICEF guidelines recommend breastfeeding babies within the first hour of birth and exclusively breastfeeding for the first six months of life – meaning no other foods or liquids, including water. The guidelines also say that babies should be breastfed on demand – that's as often as they want, day and night.

Even if the WHO hadn't recommended it, breastfeeding would still have appealed to me because of the general lack of faffing and preparation required. Breast milk is instantly available, at just the right temperature, and it's free! Plus, I heard that it can act as a natural contraceptive, which seemed like a no-brainer at the time – I wasn't ready to get pregnant again that soon, so anything that might help there was good for me! (But remember that this isn't foolproof mamas, always talk to your midwife or healthcare professional about contraception after you've given birth.) I had also read somewhere that colostrum – the thick, yellowy milk that comes out at the very start – is good for babies and contains loads of great immune-boosting nutrients that support them in the early days and weeks. (I also heard somewhere that top athletes use colostrum from cows to build strength and performance... ew!)

So here I was in the hospital, experiencing this entirely natural and yet completely bizarre thing: sitting in bed with my new baby clamped on to my left boob, the feeling of little strings somehow being pulled inside me as the milk began to flow down tubes I'd never even known were there. The midwife had just kind of plonked Beau there shortly after he arrived and he had somehow known what to do and now here we were. I couldn't really tell if I was doing it right, if it was 'working' (where were the instructions?), but we kept on with it and as they weighed him each day, the scales showed he was gaining weight – tiny little increments, fractions of pounds – and that, the midwives reassured me, was what was supposed to happen.

It felt quite emotional, like I was fulfilling some sort of destiny (my hormones were all over the place and I often found myself having these moments of profundity, which usually ended in me crying). But it was astonishing to feel this complete synchronicity and connection with my baby. I couldn't quite believe it was happening at times.

I was also surprised by how often the feeds came around at first. It felt like an almost constant rotation of feed, sleep, change and feed. Particularly because I'd had the C-section and was bed-bound for those very early days, I felt like a human vending machine, dispensing milk whenever Beau pressed the button for service. This clearly wasn't going to be a three-meals-a-day arrangement, so the near continuous feeding was a shock and felt pretty exhausting. How was I supposed to get up or get dressed or get anything else done at all?

And it was painful! It wasn't the smooth, tap-like functionality that I had anticipated; it felt more like tiny pin pricks were being made in the skin on my nipples. It brought to mind the rubber caps you used to see in the hairdresser's years ago, when they were doing your highlights. I bled quite a lot, and hard scabs, that didn't look very nice at all, formed on my nipples. Occasionally blood from my boobs would spill out of Beau's mouth, mixed up with milk. It looked terrifying. (After an initial panic call to my health visitor I was at least able to know this was my bleeding nipples, and not the terrible emergency I first imagined.)

Another time, not long after we got home, my right boob became really hot and red and sore. It had been feeling funny for a while, so I probably subconsciously used it a bit less when I fed him. I also probably favoured the left boob because that felt somehow more comfortable (apparently this is very common and many of us tend to hold our babies on that side more in the early days because they can hear our heartbeats. I love how Mother Nature has all this stuff covered!). For whatever reason, there'd been a kind of blockage and now my right boob was telling me it wasn't happy at all. I'd been warned about mastitis and as soon as the swelling happened I knew that was what it was. My health visitor suggested cool flannels and some manual pumping in the bath to get things moving again. I felt like Cleopatra, bathing in milk.

Try this natural remedy

People swear by the cabbage leaf method and applying a cabbage leaf to a swollen booby can help reduce the inflammation, thanks to the mustard oil it contains. If it has been chilled in the fridge for a few hours previously, even better, as this will help reduce the hot feeling. I tried it and, guess what? It worked!

Having scabby nipples and big, red, swollen bosoms isn't much fun at the best of times, and when you are tired and dehydrated and feeling like a lump whose only purpose is to dispense milk, it can all be quite distressing for a mama. I know occasionally it felt like too much for me, as Beau clamped on again, for what felt like his fifty-eighth feed that day.

Jade found this a difficult time as well – seeing me in pain and knowing this was a problem he definitely couldn't fix. Talking to friends, I realised it's not uncommon for partners to feel alienated and like a bit of a spare part during breastfeeding – this is very much a situation between mama and baby! But Jade was brilliant and tried as much as possible to be around when I fed. He always brought me a glass of water (it's really important to stay hydrated) and often sang a little lullaby – 'You Are My Sunshine' was our family favourite – while I was feeding; that seemed to help us all relax into it

(Jade has such a beautiful voice and I always love listening to him sing).

So breastfeeding in the early days wasn't always plain sailing, but, like everything in this job, the tough times are a phase, and they pass. As we settled into life at home, as my boobs became accustomed to their new job, as Beau grew and became more efficient at feeding, the spaces between the feeds seemed to get longer and I was able to claw back a little bit of time so I could do extravagant things like have a shower and get dressed.

Thirsty work

We all know about the importance of staying hydrated, but then a baby comes along and you can so easily forget to do simple things like drink water. If you're breastfeeding, your baby is consuming a lot of your fluids so it makes sense that you need to stay topped up, mama. Being dehydrated can make you feel tired and give you a headache – absolutely not what you need right now! Try to make a habit of pouring a glass of water just before you sit down to feed, and drink it while you are feeding your baby. Hopefully it will become second nature. As a guide you need to be drinking around ten glasses of water a day when breastfeeding, instead of the usual six to eight.

Getting Out and About

As my confidence grew and Beau seemed to settle into something resembling a schedule, I began to get out and about more and feed him on the go. I always had a scarf or a big muslin handy – not because I was particularly embarrassed, it just felt right for me. I know other people who didn't mind getting their boobs out and others who had big breastfeeding scarves to cover everything. All of these things are OK in my book, it's about whatever makes you feel comfortable. If other people want to feel scandalised or offended, that's up to them.

It is odd when you think about it, the way other people react to women feeding their babies. There's nothing more natural than a woman feeding her baby. And let's face it, it's not like a pair of boobs is anything new these days. Boobs are everywhere! But the sight of a woman breastfeeding still seems to make some people feel uncomfortable. They just don't seem to know where to look.

I remember being at a friend's wedding, on one of those late September days when the sun is blazing and no one can quite believe it's still so hot. We'd been in the garden all afternoon and Beau needed a feed so I snuck off inside to find somewhere cooler (it can all get a bit warm for you and the baby when you're feeding – all that body heat). As I sat there a man walked past, a fellow guest who I'd never met, obviously trying to find the toilet. He took a second glance as he recognised me, then came over and stood right over me, and tried to have a chat and kept looking directly at Beau as he fed. It wasn't threatening; I think he was probably just trying to be Mr Cool and let me know that he was totally down with women breastfeeding in public. But the whole thing was awkward and in the end I had to ask him politely to give me some privacy.

So much has changed since then, and so much continues to change in the world for women. All we mamas can do is keep on doing what we feel is right for us. And the more breastfeeding we do in public, the more normal it will become for everyone.

This is what we are built for, and keep on doing it, because the more we do it, the more normal it will become.

Booby Spice's top tips for breast-feeding mamas on the go

—

If you're worried about getting it wrong (like I was), about how other people will react or you just need a little confidence boost, especially when you are out and about, here are my tips to help you feel like you've got this (because you have!):

Plan ahead

It sounds obvious, but if you're going shopping or meeting a friend for coffee, just take a sec to think about where you're going and how comfortable you'll be if you need to feed your baby while you're there. Avoid cafes where you might have to sit on a high stool or an upturned barrel! You'll find the things you want from a location will change quite a lot once you've had a baby and all that cool, industrial/reclaimed furniture at your favourite hipster cafe may not cut it for the new breastfeeding you.

Other mums are always the best source of information, so it's good to ask them for advice on the best spots. Your health visitor or local children's services should also be able to help and often cafes put signs in their windows to let you know they welcome breastfeeding. If you're somewhere new, the breastfeeding location app, FeedFinder, will show you where your nearest registered cafes and restaurants are.

Know you're in the right

It is illegal for anyone to ask you not to feed in a public place or on public transport. If someone asks you to stop or to leave, you can tell them that the Equality Act 2010 states, 'a business cannot discriminate against mothers who are breastfeeding a child of any age'. That should shut them up!

Dress for the occasion

Like any activity, wearing the right clothes for you, preferably ones that make you feel both comfortable and gorgeous at the same time, can really help. What you wear is obviously down to your tastes. Some of my friends didn't mind their boobs being 'out' and wore tops with buttons that they could undo. I decided to wear big loose tops that I could lift up easily to feed. You can also get breastfeeding shawls and slings that cover your stomach and pretty much everything else, if that's your preference. It's entirely up to you. The important thing is that you feel in control.

Invest in a good maternity bra or two

A decent breastfeeding bra will become your best friend, or at least your bosom buddy. There wasn't a lot of choice just a few years ago, but these days, most of the big high-street names do lovely maternity bras that come in all sizes and have nice designs that don't look like something you've borrowed off your nan. Avoid bras with underwiring in the early months as experts say the hard materials can cause blocked ducts and mastitis. You don't have to wear a bra at all if you don't want to, but if you choose to they can be helpful for keeping breast pads in place. Plus, you'll probably find that they are the most comfortable bras you'll ever own and you'll want to wear them long after you stop breastfeeding (I wear mine in the gym)!

Don't forget the breast pads!

Simple as they are, breast pads will save you much embarrassment if you start lactating at an awkward moment, and they mean less bra-washing for you. What's not to love?

Don't fly solo

Even just popping out for a bit of shopping can feel like a massive mission when you are breastfeeding, so don't feel bad about getting someone to come with you.

Fran Bailey is a breastfeeding counsellor for the National Childbirth Trust (NCT) and has supported thousands of women on their feeding journeys with breastfeeding, bottle-feeding and early weaning. Here she goes through everything you need to know about breastfeeding.

TAKE IT FROM THE EXPERT

FRAN BAILEY – NCT
BREASTFEEDING COUNSELLOR

WHY BREASTFEED?

❝ The WHO, the NHS and UNICEF all encourage women to give their babies nothing but breast milk for the first six months of their lives. This is because of the huge positive health outcomes associated with breast milk and breastfeeding — for both mums and babies! The research shows that it is good for their immune systems — helping them to fight off illness in the early months, but also later in life — and that it is good for keeping babies' tummies healthy. The research also shows that breastfeeding can make it less likely for babies to get ear infections and it supports healthy jaw development.

Breastfeeding has been shown to reduce the likelihood of women developing certain types of cancer, it burns calories (although not as many as I always wanted it to) and can be a lovely way to bond with your baby. And, as Emma says, it is also great if you are on the go. You don't need any equipment, there are no bottles to wash and sterilise, no water to boil and you don't need to wait for it to cool to the correct temperature.

Not everyone finds it straightforward and it's really important to seek support early on if you're finding it tough. Many women find breastfeeding difficult and this can be a really miserable experience.

Sometimes women don't get the support they need or decide that breastfeeding isn't right for them, and sometimes women simply don't want to breastfeed or aren't able to. Whatever their decision and reason, women should be supported and not judged.

'Sometimes women simply
don't want to breastfeed
or aren't able to.
Whatever their decision
and reason, women
should be supported
and not judged.'

—

FRAN BAILEY

ARE YOU SITTING COMFORTABLY?

One of the most important things when you are starting out is to <u>make sure that you are comfortable.</u> It is hard to know how long each feed will last and your comfort is super important to help you feed your baby effectively.

Often women find it easiest if they are slightly leaning back in a supportive chair or in bed. Being relaxed also lets the hormones that help breastfeeding work do their thing!

Babies need to have a really big mouthful of breast to be able to feed effectively. It's helpful to remember it is 'breast' feeding, not 'nipple' feeding. Some top tips to help this work are:

- <u>Support the back of your baby's neck rather than their head</u> so they are free to tip their head backwards and your nipple is aimed to the roof of their mouth.

- Hold your baby really close to your body with their head, neck and shoulders in line – that will help your baby be comfortable throughout the feed.

- Wait until your baby opens their mouth nice and wide and then pull your baby close into the breast.

You can get some more information on this from the NCT website: nct.org.uk

HOW MUCH IS ENOUGH?

Babies tend to fall off the breast when they have had enough to eat (similarly they will turn away from a bottle or clamp their mouths shut). They will often have a very contented look about them when full, sometimes described as being in a 'milk coma' or 'milk drunk'.

Sometimes towards the end of a feed, babies will flutter a little at the breast. This doesn't necessarily mean they have finished. You might find it helpful to move your baby to the other breast at this point and encourage them to feed a little more.

Generally speaking, you can tell if they are getting enough overall by the contents of their nappies. If a baby is getting enough milk, they will produce a good number of wet nappies every day and at least one poo.

In their first forty-eight hours, your baby will probably only have two or three wet nappies. But from day five, you should get at least five or six heavy, wet nappies every twenty-four hours. Behaviour wise, a baby who is getting enough milk will have periods of being awake and asleep and will usually wake themselves up to let you know they are hungry.

It is worth remembering that initially it is very common for babies to lose up to 10 per cent of their body weight, but you will see them start to gain again after a few days and they should be back up to their birth weight within the first couple of weeks.

DON'T WORRY ABOUT A ROUTINE AT FIRST

All babies and their families are different and thrive on different ways of managing the early weeks and months. In the early days it will be easiest for you, and best for your baby and your milk production, if you feed them responsively. This means that you follow your baby's cues and, when they start to show signs of hunger (starting to wiggle around and fuss a little, turn towards the breast or start sucking on their fingers and fists), you feed them. For some mothers, their own breasts starting to tingle or feel uncomfortably full might also be signs to offer the baby the breast. <u>As a general rule, you might expect to feed a new baby about 10—12 times every 24 hours.</u>

PACED BOTTLE-FEEDING

This is a technique that mimics breastfeeding in that it allows your baby to have control of the pace and flow of the feed. In this technique, you simply pause during a bottle-feed, either by removing the bottle from their mouth completely or just tipping it slightly to stop the flow of milk, and wait to see if your baby urges you to carry on or if they are satisfied. Not only do they get to take the lead, but you avoid overfeeding and any associated problems with indigestion and taking in too much air.

Boobs, Bottles and Beyond! 71

CHECK YOUR BABY'S LATCH

If your nipples are sore and cracked it can be a sign that your baby has not latched on to the breast well for one or a few feeds. Sore, cracked nipples can be really painful and often mums say they start to dread feeding their baby. Things that can help are making sure that your baby has a really good mouthful of breast in their mouth when they feed — remember breastfeeding rather than nipple feeding!

You can get healing creams from a pharmacy and women tend to say that a pure lanolin cream works effectively as a relief. Women also find that rubbing some expressed breast milk on to the nipples and letting them air dry can really help bring relief.

SOOTHING LANOLIN

Lanolin is a super-moisturising oil found in sheep's wool. Most lanolin creams are cruelty-free, but if you want a completely vegan alternative, coconut or olive oil can help (but make sure your nipples are au naturel when it's time to feed again).

IT TAKES A WHILE FOR YOUR MILK SUPPLY TO SETTLE

Breasts can feel really full and uncomfortable in the very early days of feeding your baby, when milk changes from the initial colostrum (the amazing fluid which meets all of your new baby's feeding needs) into milk as you know it, which starts to fill the breasts around day three.

It might also happen if you have had a change to your normal feeding pattern. Many women find that hand expressing a little milk can help (see page 81), as can cooling breasts down with a cold flannel or a chilled cabbage leaf (see page 56).

FEELING UNCOMFORTABLE FEEDING IN PUBLIC IS NORMAL

Lots of women worry about feeding when they're out and about, but there are so many things that can help.

- Remember, breastfeeding women can legally feed their babies in public (see page 62). Whether bottle- or breastfeeding, it is important that mums are able to feed their baby whenever and wherever they need to.

- To build confidence, some mums start by feeding their baby at a breastfeeding drop-in or parent and baby group, where other mums are likely to be feeding too.

- Many women find that with practise they can breastfeed their baby without anyone even noticing. If you are worried, you can wear a large scarf to drape over your breast or a vest top underneath a baggy top to avoid having much skin on show.

- Lots of mothers find it useful to practise in a safe environment or in front of a mirror so they can check how much skin can be seen.

SURROUND YOURSELF WITH SUPPORT

It can feel really hard to make a decision to breast- or bottle-feed your baby if other family members or friends have made a different decision. Many women can feel pressurised to make decisions that perhaps they do not feel entirely comfortable with. This may be to do with the sense that one way of feeding your baby is preferable.

Stopping breastfeeding is also something that has to feel right for you. There are no right or wrong ways to feed your baby. However, many women feel under enormous pressure to either keep going with breastfeeding or, conversely, research indicates that huge numbers of women stop breastfeeding before they feel ready to.

Whatever feeding decision you make, it helps to have people around you who support your decision. This may be a family member or good friend, a health professional or peer support group that can help you feel more confident to feed your baby in the way you want to.

SOMETIMES BREASTFEEDING DOESN'T WORK OUT... AND THAT'S OK!

We are lucky to live in an age where we have safe alternatives to breast milk. Formula milk is designed to be safe for babies and there are strict government rules about its production and advertising.

Babies need to begin with a milk designed for newborns, often called 'first milk', and this is usually the only formula milk your baby will need until they reach 12 months old when they can move on to cow's milk.

If research has indicated that something is beneficial to babies,

it legally has to be in every infant formula milk. In other words, regardless of their cost, all brands have to meet the same nutritional and safety standards and have a relatively similar composition.

Some women make a decision to exclusively use formula milk to feed their babies, while others use it alongside either breastfeeding or expressing and using a bottle. It may take some time and some experimentation, but you will find a way that works for you and your baby.

FEEDING AND BONDING

Whether you decide to breast- or bottle-feed, it is a wonderful opportunity to bond with your baby. Lots of skin-to-skin contact, however you are feeding your baby, will help. So will eye contact, talking to and singing to your baby.

This all stimulates the motherly hormones which help you and your baby to bond with each other and enjoy being close. For many families it's best to limit the number of people giving your baby a bottle to a maximum of three, to enable your baby to build up these close bonds.

let's talk about tongue-tie

—

I'd never heard of tongue-tie until I had Tate. We tried breastfeeding straight away, just like we had with Beau, but I could tell almost immediately that the milk just wasn't going down so well. In fact, it was coming back up quite a lot, and Tate just didn't seem to latch on the way Beau did. The weight gain wasn't what it should be either, so we started combining breast- and bottle-feeds, from quite early on.

But even with the bottle, there was something unusual about the way Tate latched on. The bottle teats got squashed into all sorts of funny shapes, and there was never that sense of really having filled them up during a feed. We went through every shape and every brand trying to find one that worked. We were baffled, and a little bit worried, trying to work out what was going on.

Eventually, our doctor realised that Tate had what's called a tongue-tie. As the name suggests, it's a condition where the skin that connects the tongue to the bottom of the mouth is shorter and thicker than usual. This means a baby's tongue is less able to move around in the way they need it to for feeding (and later on, speech, as it can cause lisps and other problems with pronunciation). Underneath your baby's tongue just isn't somewhere that you see that often, so it can be hard to spot.

It's not always necessary to treat tongue-tie – it depends on how difficult it is making things. But because of the problems we were having with feeds and Tate's general unsettledness, our doctor recommended that we had the treatment, that's called a tongue-tie division or a frenulotomy. He explained that a specialist practitioner would come to the house and snip the skin that was causing the tie. When he said those words, I felt all the blood drain from my face. I couldn't bear the thought of someone doing that to my baby! I imagined blood and screams and tears. But he explained that actually it's a fairly painless procedure for babies. The skin that is snipped doesn't contain many nerve endings and some babies can actually sleep through the whole process.

Reassured, we decided to go ahead with it, as by that stage we were really worried about Tate's problems with feeding. I still locked myself away in the bathroom on the day it happened! Jade had to handle this one for us; I couldn't be in the same room while that happened to my baby. The midwife came to the house to do it, and it was all over in a few minutes. And things improved almost as quickly! Tate seemed able to get a much better grip on the boob and the bottle, and seemed more full up after a feed.

There's lots of information on the NHS website about tongue-tie (nhs.uk). If you think your baby might be suffering from a tongue-tie, your GP or health visitor will be able to help you.

Fran at the NCT has some great tips on how to express too.

EXPRESS YOURSELF!

6 Expressing breast milk is something some women find a lot easier than others. It can be extremely useful to have a back-up supply of breast milk, particularly if your baby is premature or unwell and needs to spend time away from you, or if you are going back to work but want to continue breastfeeding. It can also let your partner take part in the feeding process. However, expressing milk is not always straightforward. I've got some hints and tips to make it easier for you.

- Being relaxed when you express (just like during breastfeeding) will help the hormones that release breast milk work more effectively. Get yourself set up somewhere comfortable and have a book or a warm drink on hand to help.

- Often, expressing first thing in the morning works well, as the hormone that makes breast milk has had a chance to replenish while you've been resting overnight.

- Looking at or thinking about your baby, or even looking at a photo of them, can help to make expressing a little easier.

HOW TO EXPRESS

Some women like expressing simply by hand while others use a breast pump, either manual or electric. How you decide to express depends very much on the quantity of milk you are expressing each day and how much milk you need.

HAND EXPRESSING

Good for: small amounts of milk; to mix with food; quick and fuss-free expressing; relieving engorged breasts.

1. You'll need clean hands and a sterilised container.

2. Gently massage your breasts, working down from your armpit to your nipple (this helps stimulate your let-down reflex).

3. Cup your hands in a c-shape around the outside of your nipple, and feel for the ridge behind your nipple. Then start gently squeezing or compressing your breast.

4. It may take a few minutes so be patient! Gradually your breast milk (or colostrum) will start to slowly drip out. It can take a while to build up a flow so keep at it.

5. When you notice your milk flow slowing down, try moving your hands around your breast so you are expressing from a different area. Repeat on the other breast if required.

6. Pop a lid on the container and store your milk in the fridge, or at room temperature for up to six hours.

Boobs, Bottles and Beyond!

MANUAL PUMPING

Good for: affordability; quiet and unobtrusive;
light and easy to carry.

1. Wash your hands and make sure the pump, bottle and
   parts are clean and sterile before use. Get comfy.

2. Massage your breasts as described on page 81,
   to stimulate your let-down reflex.

3. Place the pump's funnel over your nipple, and
   slowly start to pump. It can take a few minutes
   before your milk starts flowing so don't give up!

4. Switch breasts when your flow starts slowing
   down. You might find that one breast produces
   more milk than the other — this is normal!

5. Pop a lid on the bottle and store your milk
   in the fridge, or at room temperature for up
   to six hours. Wash and sterilise your pump.

ELECTRIC PUMPING

Good for: fast, efficient pumping; reliable; does the work for you.

1. Wash your hands and make sure the pump, bottle and parts are clean and sterile before use. Get comfy.

2. Massage your breasts as described on page 81, to stimulate your let-down reflex.

3. Place the pump's funnel over your nipple, and switch the machine on. Start on the slowest speed and build up to one that is comfortable for you. You can increase the speed as your flow increases.

4. Switch breasts when your flow starts slowing down. You might find that one breast produces more milk than the other — this is normal!

5. Pop a lid on the bottle and store your milk in the fridge, or at room temperature for up to six hours. Wash and sterilise your pump.

HIRE DON'T BUY

Electric breast pumps can be really expensive so it's worth hiring one, especially if you're not sure which option is right for you. Your local breastfeeding counsellor or health visitor will be able to put you in touch with local suppliers. There are also online services that post the pumps out to you.

Leaky Moments

We started introducing bottles and formula milk to Beau at the beginning of the Spice Girls world tour. I was lucky that I could bring my baby with me to work, but, like any working mum, I still needed my partner to be able to take on some of the feeding duties so I could do my job. Luckily Beau quickly worked out that he liked the taste of formula, and switched between the breast and bottle quite happily.

It was less straightforward for me! Helping your body understand that demand for milk has decreased doesn't happen overnight, and it takes a while for a new level of production to kick in. Your boobs get engorged with the extra milk, and it can all be a bit sore if you find yourself 'feed-ready' without a baby close by to relieve you.

I have memories of lactating quite heavily during one of my first performances on that tour, at the STAPLES Center in LA. Our costumes had been designed by Roberto Cavalli, who Victoria knew, and oh my goodness they were beautiful. He had us in gorgeous gowns and tuxedos and corsets, lots of gold and silver – they were exactly the right mix of fun and grown-up glamour that we needed at that stage in our evolution. But stage costumes are different to evening wear. These were heavy, highly structured pieces (they had to withstand quite a

lot of activity!) and there were frequent changes. I remember it happened during 'Say You'll Be There' – I was wearing a rose-gold dress with an empire line and a high neck, with gold lamé that was quite close-fitting over my boobs. I had to get through a whole other track, 'Headlines', just hoping nothing was showing. As it ended I came running off stage screaming at Jade, 'Babes, get the pads! Get the pads!' Luckily, as it turns out, gold lamé isn't very porous and most of the milk had just drizzled down my stomach. But anyone looking close enough would definitely have been able to spot wet patches on my boobs during that number.

I can look back and smile about it now, but when I look at the pictures I also see a woman who really wasn't ready to be throwing herself into that kind of physically demanding regime. I absolutely love being a Spice Girl and performing; some of my happiest moments in life have been on stage with those girls and

Beau joining me on stage

I have memories of lactating quite heavily during one of my first performances on tour

I never forget what a privilege it is to be able to call it my work. But I simply hadn't understood the huge processes that my body would be going through after birth and, in particular, how breastfeeding would require so much energy. They say it burns around 300 calories a day, which I'm sure it does, because it takes a lot of power and strength to keep producing all that nutritious milk. To try to combine that with an energetic stage tour and sleepless nights was, with the benefit of hindsight, not a great idea. There were a lot of tears and a fair amount of self-recrimination. (And it didn't help that a particularly unkind corner of the UK press felt the need to say vile things about my thighs on that tour, either. Body-shaming: you'd never hear blokes doing that to each other shortly after they've had a baby.)

It wasn't all bad though! I was, for the most part, extremely happy to be able to share some of the feeding load with Jade at last, to reclaim some precious minutes of the day for myself, feel less like a milk machine or have a glass of wine if I wanted to. It was also just lovely to watch Jade feeding him. It made me realise how small Beau was! From this entirely new angle, in his daddy's big arms, my baby looked extra-tiny and even more precious.

But the Mama Bear in me also felt a sadness about letting go of those feeds. It had been such a bonding experience, and I knew it was time with Beau that I wouldn't get back. Luckily, motherhood has a way of giving as she takes away. Before I could get too misty-eyed about breastfeeding Beau, it was time to start weaning, and oh my goodness did that keep me busy.

Introducing solid food is an interesting time for everyone
and Fran has some excellent information to help with weaning
too – thanks Fran!

TAKE IT FROM THE EXPERT

FRAN BAILEY - NCT
BREASTFEEDING COUNSELLOR

INTRODUCING SOLIDS

NHS guidelines say that babies should not be
moved on to solid foods until they are around
six months old.

Sometimes you might think your baby is ready
for food earlier than this because they show
an interest in what the adults around them are
eating. However, babies are fascinated by lots
of things around them, so it's helpful to know
some of the other signs to look out for.

You really need to be looking for three key developmental stages to know if your baby is ready for the next phase:

1. <u>Can your baby sit up without support</u> and do they have good back, neck and head control.

2. <u>Can your baby grasp things</u> and move them from their hands to their mouth, as you might notice them do with toys?

3. <u>Has your baby lost their 'tongue reflex'</u> that was present at birth? In other words, can your baby start to move food from the front to the back of their mouth?

There is much more to be said about introducing solids and you can get lots of information on the NCT and NHS websites, among other places. Once you have established that your baby is ready for solids, the feeding fun really begins!

Giving Beau and Tate their first taste of solid foods was such good fun. Messy! But fun. I loved seeing their faces when they tried new flavours. There is no one more honest than a baby when it comes to expressing their likes and dislikes. Watching them register the sweetness of a raspberry or the warmth of some homely mashed potato was always such a joy.

It can all feel quite daunting when you start to think about weaning; knowing when to do it and how much to give them, what they can and can't eat, and how much milk they still need. Oh, and their nappies can be quite a shock! Especially if they've been eating bananas – you'll find little black seeds in their poop!

There was, and still is, a lot of talk about baby-led weaning, where you let your baby feed themselves, versus spoon-feeding. Baby-led weaning is based on the idea that babies can and should feed themselves with their hands when they are able to do so, thereby setting their own pace and learning to differentiate between foods. You basically give them soft finger foods they can pick up themselves and let them get to work. Unsurprisingly, it can be very messy! And to begin with you may find that not a lot of food actually gets ingested, as your baby will be more interested in exploring the textures and seeing what happens when they throw it on the floor!

The more traditional method of feeding your baby with a spoon usually means puréeing their food before offering it to them. You have more control over what they eat this way and, while it's still usually very messy, it's not quite in the same league as baby-led weaning.

Weaning was messy, but so much fun. I loved seeing their little faces when they tried new flavours.

As always, for me it was about doing a bit of everything. If I was at home and had the time I would steam some veg and chop up some soft fruit and let them pick up the pieces themselves. Sometimes at breakfast I made scrambled eggs or porridge fingers (porridge left to cool and sliced into fingers they could pick up and munch on). But if I was watching the clock, or needed to know that they had really eaten a proper meal, I would use a spoon to feed them.

How you decide to wean your baby is of course entirely up to you. Luckily, there is tons of information out there about how to do it (the NHS Start4Life has all the best up-to-date information), and quite a few of my favourite television chefs have published books about weaning as well, so I know you will have plenty of reliable resources to help you make the right choices. Just make sure you follow Fran's advice about knowing when they are ready, and remember that weaning is a gradual process. You really don't need to rush this one. Trust me, before you know it they'll be eating you out of house and home, even if they are a bit fussy at first!

Luckily for me, I have a partner who also happens to be an amazing chef, so when it came to weaning I was more than happy to let Jade take the lead. He whizzed up loads of delicious purées and often made meals for us grown-ups that could be mashed or puréed, so the babies were having the same as us.

And because Jade is half British-Jamaican, he made sure they developed a taste for Caribbean flavours early on. To this day, the kids' favourite dinner is chicken and rice, and I have to ask for mine not to be as spicy as theirs!

Here are a few tips from Jade on weaning, and a favourite family recipe for you to try if you fancy it...

A little something from Jade, our head chef

—

‘ For a chef like me, a baby is the ultimate customer because they don't come with any preconceived ideas about what they do and don't like! They don't know if they hate basil or love banana, so you can really have fun with feeding them (as long as it's safe, of course). I gave our kids a whole range of tastes and textures from early on, and I'm proud that both of them are still what my mum would call 'good eaters'.

Even from when they were just starting to try solid foods, I tried to make sure we were all sitting down together at mealtimes. (We had those high chairs that pull up to the table so they were both sitting at the table with us for meals.) Just sharing the experience of eating together is so important and something we still try to do every day. We started out, like most people, with baby rice and moved on to things like stewed fruit or root vegetables – carrots and sweet potatoes were always a favourite – and I used herbs and spices to give them more flavour and interest (just go easy at first, and remember babies don't need salt!).

One of my favourite things to give them when they were starting to feed themselves a bit was plantain, a kind of banana that's used a lot in Jamaican cooking. You just peel the plantain, slice it lengthways into fingers and bake for 10 minutes on each side. This makes great finger food for them to suck on and dip into a purée or mashed veggies.

Another thing we used to do (when weaning had been established, don't do this until you have a confident eater) was steam peas so they were really soft, and put them out on their little tray during dinner time. The precision required for them to pick up the peas is great for their pincer grip and focus, and you get a couple of minutes to wolf down your own dinner while they are trying to chase the peas!

As they got a bit older, I loved making my mild coconut chicken curry for us all. Obviously I wouldn't put too much spice in at the beginning, but I would still put some in to get them used to it. It never hurt me! Turn over for the recipe.

Top Tip

According to the NHS, you can safely add gentle spices to weaning recipes from six months onwards. It makes food more interesting for baby and helps them develop wider tastes.

Boobs, Bottles and Beyond!

Jade's Coconut Chicken Curry with Squash

SERVES A HUNGRY FAMILY OF FOUR

8 skinless and boneless chicken thighs, cut into chunks

4 tbsp mild curry powder

2 tbsp allspice

2 sprigs of thyme, leaves picked

2 tbsp fresh root ginger, peeled and minced

3 garlic cloves, grated or crushed

1 tbsp coconut oil, for sautéing

2 onions, finely chopped

2 x 400ml tins coconut milk

1 large potato, peeled and diced

1 small butternut squash, peeled and diced

salt to taste (after separating the kids' serving)

1. Put the chicken in a non-metallic mixing bowl. Take half of all the spices, herbs, ginger and garlic, and rub all over the chicken. Cover and leave to marinate for at least an hour (or overnight for maximum flavour).

2. Melt the coconut oil over a low heat, and add the onions with the rest of the spices, herbs, ginger and garlic. Sauté until soft.

3. Add the chicken to the sautéed onions and cook until the meat is sealed, then add the coconut milk, potatoes and squash. Bring to the boil and simmer for 25–30 minutes or until the chicken, potatoes and squash are cooked. The slower and longer you cook this dish the more flavoursome it is.

4. Season to taste (adults only!) and serve with rice for the grown-ups and older kids, and blend to a purée for your baby (you can add a little milk or water if you think it needs loosening up).

Night-Time Reading

ALL ABOUT SLEEP – AND WHEN IT'S NOT HAPPENING

Chapter Three

Sleep is one of those things
that everyone wants to talk
about when you have a baby...

Even while I was pregnant, I noticed that a lot of other mums
liked to offer me their advice about my forthcoming sleep
problems (usually a variation on 'Make sure you sleep when
they sleep!' or 'Just go to bed at 5pm!'). The general consensus
seemed to be that if you could get the baby's sleep sorted out,
everything else would fall into place. This made perfect sense
to me, as sleep deprivation is an actual form of torture, and
avoiding torture is pretty much always a good idea in my book.

   Although I didn't really know what getting it sorted
out meant at that point – what did a good sleeper look like
anyway? A baby who slept regularly or a baby who slept for
ages, or both?

I felt quietly confident about the sleep issue because I've always been quite proud of my own ability to sleep whenever and wherever the urge takes me, so the idea of sleeping when my baby slept didn't worry me. I am officially very good at grabbing forty winks!

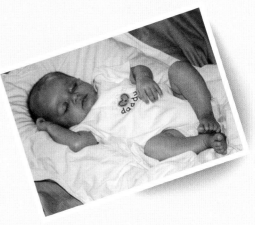

However, I know that this is not the case for lots of women. While daytime napping wasn't an issue for me, the night time was another situation altogether that I wasn't prepared for!

Whatever your sleep experience in those early weeks, the thing everyone has said to me, and I found too, is that, once you become a parent, you never sleep the same ever again!

I lost count of the number of times people asked me if I was getting sleep or if my baby was a 'good sleeper'.

As far back as I can remember, I've always been able to snooze when I needed to. But then all those years of long nights in the studio and on tour really fine-tuned my sleeping prowess. As Spice Girls we all had to learn the art of sleeping on the go, but the others would still marvel at how, on any flight, I would be out like a light before we'd even taken off. If we were recording, it would often happen in the evening, and, whenever there was a break, I would happily take myself off and catch some Zs on a sofa or in an armchair somewhere. I never needed sleep masks or pillow mist or ear plugs or any of those things to help me drift off, either. And, to this day, I usually prefer some light in my bedroom rather than complete darkness.

Did you know?

—

Women need an average of 20 minutes more sleep a day than men. Sleep neuroscientists at Loughborough University's Clinical Sleep Research Unit found out that because women multitask and generally use their brains more than men during the day, we need to rest them for longer at night. Keep that one up your sleeve for the next time you need a lie-in.

So when people told me I'd need to learn to sleep when the baby slept, I didn't worry too much about it; I was already an expert in this field. To some extent I think I did cope pretty well – in the daytime at least. When they slept during the day, I would try my hardest to close my eyes on the sofa and drift off. I've even been known to have a little doze on the driveway, in the car, while they were asleep in the back. So if I felt tired during the day I generally had no problem grabbing a power nap.

What I wasn't prepared for was the lying awake at night, unable to sleep because I was listening to the baby's breathing or watching them to check they were OK. Or only sleeping in a kind of shallow, half-sleep that wasn't really sleep so much as keeping my eyes closed while my thoughts zoomed all over the place. Or waking up seconds before the baby woke up, like when you wake up just before your alarm and feel really cheated out of those extra few minutes. Or obsessively watching the baby monitor for the slightest movement. Often it wasn't the baby's lack of sleep keeping me awake, but my own hyper vigilance.

Method to the madness

—

Many scientists and psychologists believe that babies are actually programmed to keep us busy at night, even if they're not feeling unwell. The theory goes that keeping us up, especially if we are breastfeeding them, ensures we are a) awake and not vulnerable to predators, and b) unlikely to get pregnant any time soon (and give our attentions to a new imposter baby), since breastfeeding is a kind of natural contraceptive. Yes, keeping us up all night is an evolutionary survival tactic – clever babies! It's good to know they're not just doing it for a laugh, but also a hard one to really get behind when it's 4.17am and you have had precisely 30 minutes of sleep (and there is literally no chance anyone is having any sex anyway).

Night-Time Reading

Don't Mess with Mama Bear

Why was it so difficult to relax when they slept at night-time? I had some real Mama Bear stuff going on! I felt so attached and protective of them (in fact, I still do – I find myself welling up sometimes when they go to school, as if they are going away for a whole term and not until 3.30pm that afternoon). I felt very strongly this overwhelming instinct to stay close by; I needed them to know that I was there when they went to sleep, and that I'd be there when they woke up in the night. And so I was, even though at times it felt like I was in a real-life nightmare, hauling myself up in bed, fumbling around in the dark for whichever boob needed emptying first, making sure it was ready for action (eventually I devised a system where I put a breast pad on the boob I'd fed with last so I knew which one was up next). I remember Geri telling me, before Beau arrived, that those moments in the middle of the night, when it is just you and your baby, are some of the most magical you experience as a mum. And they were. But oh my goodness, like so much of this baby game, it was the most precious and beautiful thing ever, while simultaneously being the hardest.

Both of my babies did a very good job of keeping me awake when they wanted to, and each in their own unique way. I know I had it easier than a lot of my friends – Jade jokes that the children must have inherited my magical sleep powers – but they were still not always that keen to go to sleep! Beau definitely didn't agree with us about what constituted night-time, and would often be wide-eyed and ready to play at 11pm, or chuckling away to himself with his little legs racing in the air in the early hours, for no apparent reason.

When Tate came along, we found ourselves dealing with the whole new world of pain that is acid reflux. Like indigestion or heartburn, reflux happens when semi-digested milk comes back up the food pipe. It's quite common in young babies because the muscles at the base of their oesophagus haven't fully developed yet. If they've got it you'll notice your baby spitting up milk and phlegm after a feed and generally being a bit cross about it. Things get particularly problematic at night-time for a baby with reflux, because it is all happening while they are flat on their backs in a cot, in the dark.

I can't tell you anything nice about reflux – it was distressing for us and obviously for Tate, who was a little trooper, but often really uncomfortable with it all. The sound of the crying as it intensified has stayed with me ever since. The only good thing about reflux is you know they will eventually grow out of it as their food pipe develops, usually within the first six months. And that's exactly what happened!

Many a time I waved Jade off as he put the car seat in the car to drive around the block and try to make one of them finally drift off. And I got muscles like Popeye from doing the 'mum sway' at all hours – that gentle side-to-side movement all mothers seem to do instinctively when holding their babies (and I've since noticed, other people's babies!). It seems to mimic the sensation of being in the womb and reassures them, especially if you are holding them close and they can hear your heartbeat. Ahhh.

I got muscles like Popeye from doing the 'mum sway' at all hours.

I tried dummies with my babies and they worked with one and not the other. Beau loved a dummy and it really settled him at night in his cot but Tate didn't need one or get on with dummies at all.

TAKE IT FROM THE EXPERT

DR CRAIG CANAPARI –
PAEDIATRIC SLEEP CONSULTANT

WILL A DUMMY HELP MY BABY SLEEP?

'Dummies are known as pacifiers in the US. They are safe to use in the first several years of life, and there is little to no evidence of harm provided that your child stops using it by three years of age, although many children stop beforehand. Helping your baby to settle and drift off to sleep with a dummy during the first year won't cause sleep or nursing problems. They also seem to reduce the risk of cot death, so the American Academy of Pediatrics encourages dummy use at least in the first six months of life. It is usually easy to get rid of it after six to nine months of age if you wish, but it is fine to continue it up to three years of age without any ill effects on your child's teeth. '

Moving Out Time

We moved both babies into their own rooms when they were about six months old. (In the UK, NHS guidelines state babies should sleep in the same room as you until they are at least this age. Although incredibly rare, most infant deaths happen in the first six months so it makes sense that you are close by during this time. And, of course, it helps your baby feel secure and safe in the night in those early months, while they are still acclimatising to life outside the womb. It's also just easier when you are feeding so frequently.)

It was a mixed up time for me, emotionally. On the one hand I knew we had to get them used to sleeping in their own rooms, and that being in the quiet of their own space might help all of us get some longer stretches in (lying awake all those nights I realised it's surprisingly noisy when there are three of you in a room, even if two of you are asleep). But on the other hand, especially when it was time to move Tate, I felt such a tug. My babies were growing up!

And while I wanted them, and us, to find that tiny bit of independence, at the same time part of me was frightened about leaving them on their own. It wasn't necessarily a rational fear – this was more a kind of primal instinct that I couldn't shake. While I had to concede that the threat of wolves eating them in the night was relatively low, it still felt

counter-intuitive somehow to be apart from them, even if they were only in the next room, literally a couple of metres away.

This was when I realised that there are many, many gadgets out there that play on parents' anxieties by offering us solutions to the problems we didn't know we had. We'd already been using a video monitor that I kept with me while they slept during the day. It meant that when they made a noise in their sleep, I could see quite quickly if it was a waking-up kind of noise or just a momentary snuffle. This seemed like a good idea as it meant that Jade and I could get on with work or watch something on TV together or do whatever we needed to do, but still be there in a flash if they woke up.

Then someone told me about a 'smart' mat I could put in the cot, that would tell me via an app if the baby's heart rate changed or their breathing stopped or their body temperature dropped, and seemingly every other possible bodily function that they experienced. And for a moment I was in! What a genius idea! It was practically a guarantee that they would be 100 per cent safe while I wasn't next to them. But thankfully Jade talked me out of this particular purchase. As he pointed out, we would drive ourselves crazy checking the app all day. A constant stream of information and numbers about their every breath wouldn't necessarily give us more comfort; in fact, it might actively make us more stressed and anxious.

So many of the products aimed at new parents seem to promise us reassurance, while actually giving us the opposite. There are some really useful and important things out there for parents and babies, but beware anything that scares you or makes you doubt your own powerful instincts. In the end we decided that nothing is more natural than a sleeping baby, and the best thing we could do for them and their health was to let them sleep, without their cot being Bluetooth-enabled.

That doesn't mean to say we didn't make sure their sleeping space was safe and secure. We followed all the advice, keeping their cots fuss-free with just a flat mattress and cotton sheet. The cosy-lover in me so wanted to make it look more comfy and softer around the edges with bumpers and nice blankets, but we knew that the official guidelines say these are a no-no until they move into their first proper bed. We also made sure we had the room at the right temperature (16–20°C). Without a room thermometer I would never have got that right! And we had those brilliant little baby sleeping bags with arm holes that meant they couldn't wiggle down under the covers and risk overheating.

So with all the guidelines being safely adhered to, we tried to make the transition to full nights in their own room go smoothly. We spent lots of time in there with them during the day; all the nappy changing gear was in there and their clothes, and we put them down in there for naps when we could, so that they felt comfortable and familiar in that space.

We also made a point of doing bath time at the same time and in the same way every evening, creating that all-important sense of routine and what the experts call 'sleep cues' (those regular habits and procedures that indicate to your baby that daytime is coming to an end). There was a warm glowing night light and a lovely musical mobile that played 'You Are My Sunshine' while little elephants circled round overhead. (Sometimes we even played classical music in there! We'd gotten into the habit of playing a bit of Mozart to them when I was pregnant because I read somewhere it makes them brainy! They definitely responded to it when they were in the womb and we grew quite fond of it as a result, so sometimes we played it before bedtime.) Literally all the things that were supposed to make drifting off and staying asleep as achievable as possible were in place. But it was still a bumpy ride.

They had been used to falling asleep close to me and in our room, usually with their dad there too, bringing me a glass of water or getting the feeding pillow into just the right position for me. I never had to force Jade to be awake for those feeds; I think it was such a bonding experience for all of us, he didn't want to miss out.

But now in their own rooms the night-time feeds were meant to be more brisk and efficient (i.e. not something worth staying awake for) and neither of them appreciated this new world order much at first. I would go in and feed, put the baby back in the cot and try to sneak out. Often I'd think I had pulled it off and feel really pleased with myself, only to hear the cry start. Little puffs of indignation at first, realising they had been so rudely left in their cot, building up to the full wail if I didn't get back in there immediately. My instinct, of course, was to get back in there immediately! But very quickly this resulted in me spending most of the night awake, creeping in and out of the baby's room, repeating the same fruitless escape routine.

Even after just a few nights of this, I felt more tired than I had ever felt in my life. I was a real-life zombie and all my co-ordination seemed to have left me. I literally fell out of my bed one morning shortly after we had moved Tate! I remember saying to Jade that I MUST have been more tired than this on tour at some point, surely? But it turns out that plain old normal tiredness, from not enough sleep or physical exertion, is tiredness for beginners. Not until you have experienced the kind of profound exhaustion you feel when you're coping with a young baby who doesn't sleep through the night, can you really say that you are tired.

US Midwife Diana Spalding is a passionate advocate for giving new mamas the rest and recuperation they need. Here she explains postpartum fatigue and tired-mum syndrome, why it happens and what you can do about it:

TAKE IT FROM THE EXPERT

DIANA SPALDING –
NURSE-MIDWIFE AND
PAEDIATRIC NURSE

Two phenomena define the first year of motherhood:

1. The awe of getting to know your amazing new baby.

2. Exhaustion.

And goodness, can the exhaustion be fierce. A number of factors contribute to this, and they go beyond the obvious sleep deprivation caused by waking up with a newborn repeatedly at night — although that is certainly a big part.

To start with, you are recovering from arguably the most intense physical thing your body has ever done. You may also be breastfeeding, which requires a significant amount of physical energy. While people often say that it takes six to eight weeks to recover from pregnancy and birth, the truth is that it takes quite a bit longer — upwards of a year — to fully recover. So it stands to reason that you are going to feel tired as your body puts all that work into healing.

Another very important consideration is what's happening in the brain of a new mother. Our brains are often on high-alert; while this is very helpful from an evolutionary perspective, it can be pretty tiring to live through.

There are also emotional changes that are significant. Most new mothers experience the baby blues, a two- to three-week period just after birth in which we have big emotional swings; this is normal, but tiring. If you find that the big emotions, especially sadness or worry or mania, last longer than a few weeks, or if you find that you are unable to function as normal, feel like hurting yourself or the baby (or quite frankly, if you have any concerns about your mental well-being at all), seek help. Postpartum mental health conditions

are common, not your fault and treatable. You
are not alone, and you deserve care.

In addition to postpartum mood disorders,
there are other medical conditions that could
make you feel tired, such as anaemia and
thyroid issues. Before dismissing your fatigue
as normal, it's always a good idea to check in
with your doctor, just to make sure. Once you
have gotten the all-clear from your provider,
here are a few ideas to try to help you feel
better in yourself.

If you take one thing away from this section,
please let it be this: The perfect mother does
not exist, except to one person — your baby.
To your baby, you are perfect just the way
you are (perceived shortcomings and
all). Ignore the cultural pressures
to achieve the unattainable.
Treat yourself with the love you
deserve. If all you do on any given day
is sleep and eat and snuggle your baby, you
have done enough. You are enough — don't ever
forget it.

A big part of treating yourself with love
is allowing yourself to rest — to truly rest,
guilt-free. Despite what our go-go-go society
has led us to believe, rest is productive! So
many vital restorative functions happen in our

bodies when we are asleep (especially when we are recovering from pregnancy and birth). So take every opportunity you can, and rest. Rest when the baby sleeps, rest when your partner or family member offers to help, and rest even when you feel guilty for resting (rest especially then). <u>Rest is not a luxury, it's a necessity.</u> And know that even if rest comes in little pockets (thirty minutes here, two hours there), it's still beneficial.

Be kind to your body. We expect women to 'bounce back' after giving birth — to lose the baby weight and get straight back to normal life. This isn't realistic and it isn't fair.

To want to feel comfortable in your body is completely understandable and you get to be the boss of what that means for you. But to the extent that you can, see if you can focus on nourishing your body rather than depriving it. Eat delicious foods that will help you heal, make breast milk (if that's what you are choosing to do) and maintain your energy levels. I love:

- avocados

- oats

- salmon

- nuts

- veggies

- fruits

- eggs

- chocolate (yes, chocolate)

Hydration is also super important:

- water

- coconut water

- tea

- juice

- whatever tastes great and you enjoy drinking.

To do the things you have done (and will
continue to do) is to be a superhero; there's
no way around it. But you are also a human who
deserves rest, nourishment and love. So while
you spend time marvelling at your baby, make
sure to marvel at yourself, too. You are
absolutely amazing. Treat yourself accordingly. **,**

Helping Them Sleep through the Night

It quickly became clear that looking and feeling like a zombie is not a winning strategy for a productive life, particularly if you are a performing artist. With further tours and albums planned in the coming years, I knew I'd need to establish some kind of reasonable sleep routine so that I could return to work (aka the global stage) feeling at least partially alive.

I had heard people talk about sleep training. It sounded all wrong, to be training a baby. Would the baby be in a tracksuit and would we be blowing whistles and shouting commands? A quick online search and I realised that the Internet is awash with parents trying to work out how to help their babies sleep through the night, and everyone has an opinion about how to do it. In fact, there are some very strong opinions out there, and a lot of people not being very nice to each other about it at all (presumably because they are all so tired).

My advice is to stay away from Internet forums and anyone who thinks they have all the answers or is telling you what a bad parent you are for trying to get some sleep. Instead inform yourself of the facts, and work out a way to approach this that you feel comfortable with, that matches your instincts and gut feelings, as a mother. You might be the kind of person who doesn't like letting your baby cry for too long and would rather go in and soothe them when they wake, or you might be someone who has no problem with letting them bawl for a bit if you know it's only for a night or two. The point is that no single approach works for everyone and you have to do what feels right for you and your family.

I also found it was useful to think of this as helping, even teaching, the babies to sleep, rather than training them. We needed to help Beau, and later on Tate, get used to the idea that, for most of us, night-time is for sleeping. If we didn't teach them, how would they find this out?

For us, success (or a glimmer of it) came in a version of what's known as the 'pick up, put down' method. It works pretty much exactly how it sounds: if they are crying (and you're sure it's not time for a feed or they need a nappy change), you go into their room and pick them up to soothe them for a bit, then when they are calm you put them back in the cot. And you basically keep doing this until they go to sleep. As we'd been picking up already without much success, we sometimes replaced the picking up with simply placing a hand on their chest or leg, to let them know we were there, and keeping it there until they drifted off. This seemed like less upheaval all round, and offered fewer opportunities for accidentally rousing them as you put them back down. It didn't work all the time, and it required a will of steel and the patience of a saint at times. I know for a fact I couldn't have done it without Jade. If he hadn't been there being rational and just slightly less tired than me, I think I would have cracked more easily and had them in my room or slept in theirs, just for some peace and quiet. (Confession: Nine years later we still occasionally wake up with Tate in our bed!).

That was what worked for us, but a different way might work better for you. There are methods that involve sitting next to the cot in a chair (I tried this one too!), leaving them to cry it out, going in to console them but leaving while they are still crying, going in to console them but only leaving when they are not crying, and what's referred to as 'bedtime fading'.

Whichever way you choose to handle the sleep arrangements with your little one, it's always worth remembering that sleep is really important for all of us, and that teaching your child how to nod off easily, without you being there, is a skill they'll need pretty much their whole life. Especially if they grow up to be a pop star!

When it comes to helping your baby sleep through the night, there's no one-size-fits-all approach. But there are a few tricks and some universal truths about how to approach it that can really help us all. Dr Craig Canapari is a US paediatric sleep consultant and father of two. Here he shares his wisdom:

TAKE IT FROM THE EXPERT

DR CRAIG CANAPARI –
PAEDIATRIC SLEEP CONSULTANT

SLEEP IN THE FIRST YEAR OF LIFE

‘Any parent of a new baby can tell you that there are two surprising things about the way their new bundle of joy sleeps.

First, they sleep a surprising amount in a 24-hour period (between 14 and 16 hours is fairly typical in the first 3 months of life, with 12–15 hours being typical for the rest of the first year). Second, they usually do not do it at convenient times, or in a row, in the first few months. Sleep patterns can be quite

variable in the first few months, which is very
frustrating for sleep-deprived parents.

Sleep, like eating or breathing, is critical
to the health and development of your baby.
During sleep, children are actually learning
via a process called 'memory consolidation'.
Their brains are secreting growth hormone
so that they can get bigger and stronger.

In early infancy, babies typically need to wake
every two to four hours to feed; there seems
to be little predictability. By three to four
weeks of age, most babies have organised into
a three-hour cycle comprised of waking, feeding
and sleeping.

It's not until four to six months of age that
most babies are able to sleep through the
night (meaning that they can sleep for eight
to ten hours for a stretch). For the rest of
the first year, if you are lucky, your baby will
sleep through the night most nights, perhaps
awakening once to feed.

Breast-fed babies typically need a night feed
through to around nine months of age, whereas
formula-fed babies commonly have uninterrupted
sleep from six months of age. This is because it
takes longer to digest formula than breast milk.

A TIMELINE OF SLEEP IN THE FIRST YEAR:

AGE	SLEEP NEEDS (TOTAL)	NAP PATTERN	NOTES
Newborn (0–3 months)	14–17 hours but can be more or less	Every 1–2 hours	60% of sleep occurs during the night and 40% during the day
Infant (4–11 months)	12–16 hours	3–4 hours per day	Naps decrease from 4–5 per day to 1–2 per day; many infants take very short naps multiple times per day, even at 9–10 months
Toddler (1–2 years)	11–14 hours	2–3 hours per day	Naps decrease from 2 to 1 per day around 18 months of age

SAFE SLEEP

'Sudden infant death syndrome (SIDS), or
cot death, is a scary topic for new parents.
Fortunately, there is much you can do to
avoid it. Ensuring that your baby's sleeping
environment is safe is critical in the first year.

The recommendation is that infants room-share,
but do not bed-share, for the first six months
of age (one year in the US).

Your baby should sleep on a firm surface in
a cot, Moses basket or co-sleeper without any
soft pillows, loose blankets, cot bumpers or
stuffed animals.

Put them to sleep on their back. (Once they
can roll over, they are allowed to choose their
own sleeping position.)

I know that you can be exhausted in the first
months, but it's critical to avoid falling
asleep with your baby on surfaces like sofas
or chairs as the risk of accidental suffocation
is high.

It's better to put your baby down and let
them cry than to put them in danger by falling
asleep holding them.

BEDTIME ROUTINES

Starting a bedtime routine is one of the best things you can do to help your baby learn good sleep habits. A good routine doesn't need to be complicated. It's critical that all the grown-ups in your house can 'do' bedtime. Having only one parent able to put a child to sleep is a ticket to burnout. Bath, a story or two, a song and some cuddling are all you need. <u>Consistency is key — doing the same activities, in the same sequence, sends a calming signal to your baby that it is time for sleep.</u>

It can be tricky to find the best time to put your baby down at night. Infants who take a late afternoon nap (say, 4 to 6pm) may go to bed as late as 9 or 10pm. A good rule of thumb is that your baby will probably sleep three to four hours after their last nap ends, but you may need to experiment, adjusting your baby's nap and bedtime schedule to see what works best.

In the first few months, just soothe your baby to sleep before you put them down. Nurse, feed or rock your baby to sleep. Around three to four months, your baby starts to evolve the capacity to fall asleep independently. This is a good time to put down your baby drowsy but awake. If you are feeding or nursing your baby to sleep, you may wish to give feeding an earlier slot in the bedtime sequence. Doing so can give the non-nursing partner an opportunity to take the lead on bedtime. It's normal for your baby to fuss a bit. If they cry hysterically, however, they may not be ready yet. Try again in a week or two.

Around this time, it's also good to wait a bit before rushing to your baby if you hear them stirring at night. They may fall asleep without you being involved, which will help them continue to learn to sleep independently. Although you may want to rush to them immediately at the first cry, doing so teaches them that they need you to go back to sleep.

SIBLINGS WHO SHARE A ROOM

Twins are certainly challenging for new parents. The best thing you can do is get your children on the same schedule as quickly as possible. You may need all hands on deck at bedtime, and it's common to have to supplement with formula, depending on your milk supply.

If you have an older child, you may want to have them help with bedtime, provided that they aren't being disruptive. Alternatively, give them a quiet activity to perform while you are putting down your baby.

WHAT IF YOUR BABY IS STILL HAVING PROBLEMS SLEEPING?

Of course, things don't always go as smoothly as you would like. If your baby continues to wake up frequently after a few months of age, there are a few things you should consider.

Medical issues can certainly cause difficulty with sleep in infancy:

- Dry itchy skin can occur with eczema and can cause disrupted sleep. So can a nappy rash.

- Frequent vomiting, constipation or difficulty with growth can all suggest a feeding problem.

- Snoring, coughing or wheezing can interfere with sleep.

All of these issues should be discussed with your doctor.

IS 'SLEEP TRAINING' NECESSARY?

Think of this simply as teaching your child to fall asleep and stay asleep without you present. If you are struggling with sleep deprivation, it's definitely worth considering.

There are two different techniques that work well with infants and young children (see page 130). Regardless of the technique you choose, there is strong evidence that both techniques are safe and effective. It will not hurt your baby or your bond with your baby.

WHEN TO START A SLEEP ROUTINE

Ideally you should wait until your baby is at least six months old, and preferably no longer feeding during the night. However, if your child is still feeding multiple times during the night and is over six months of age, that could be part of the problem!

No matter how or when you decide to proceed, you first want to make sure that you have a consistent bedtime routine, and that you are committed to the technique you have selected for at least a few weeks. Don't start if you have planned a trip or expect other disruption during this period.

'A good rule of thumb is that your baby will probably sleep three to four hours after their last nap ends, but you may need to experiment, adjusting your baby's nap and bedtime schedule to see what works best.'

—

DR CRAIG CANAPARI

TWO SLEEP TECHNIQUES TO TRY

The two techniques I recommend, and that I have seen the most success with, are 'crying it out', also known as 'extinction' training, and 'camping out', also known as gradual withdrawal of parental presence. They are very different, to give you two options, depending on what feels best for you and your baby.

Crying it out

Crying it out is the most famous technique. Place your baby down to sleep drowsy but awake, and leave the room. Then keep checking on your baby at set intervals while they are crying. Checks should be brief and to the point; picking up your child, spending too much time hovering over the cot or otherwise offering more contact than a quick soothing word can be counterproductive.

Some babies find these brief checks soothing and will go to sleep more quickly. Others will redouble their crying as soon as their parents leave the room. Parents need to make a judgement about whether or not checking in is helping their baby through this process. If you decide to use checks, I recommend checking no more than every five minutes and resisting the temptation to check if your child seems to be calming down. A recent study showed that this technique results in an average of 45 minutes of crying, most typically on the first night. After a week, the amount of crying is down to almost nothing.

Camping out

Camping out involves gradually withdrawing your presence from your child's room over the course of a week or two. This method is a good fit for parents who are not comfortable with prolonged crying, although it is important to recognise that, for some children, there is no such thing as a 'no-cry' solution.

Camping out takes longer than crying it out. Every night you stay in your child's room while they fall asleep, but you gradually move away. Start by rocking your baby to sleep (or whatever usually soothes them best), then, a few nights later, put them down and rub their backs to let them know you are there and close by. A few nights later, stand or sit by the cot without touching your baby. Every few nights move your chair closer to the door. Then outside it.

DON'T FEEL GUILTY

Many parents feel guilty when they are struggling with their child's sleep. It's OK to work towards better sleep for you and your family. Sleep training, setting a sleeping routine, is safe and effective, no matter what others say online in the crankier corners of the Internet.

Likewise, don't feel like you have to sleep train if you, your partner and your baby are happy with the current arrangement, provided that you are following the safe sleep guidelines. 9

Night-Time Reading

Bath time!

—

Not all babies love bath time. A good friend's son used to
scream and wail all the way through his bath and it was all
quite distressing for her and him! He didn't seem to like
the noise of the water coming out of the taps and hated any
water going on his head. She tried all sorts of games and
jugs and toys but, in the end, it was giving him a bath in the
kitchen sink – a 'tub wash' – that worked. There was obviously
something about being at that height that made him feel much
more secure.

Both of my kids loved bath time from the word go, and
because they enjoyed it so much, we loved it too. It's such a
great way to bring the day to a close (although as they got a bit
older we did sometimes also do bath time in the day if it was
cold outside! They had ducks and boats and waterfalls going,
it was a great time-waster). This lovely family ritual has stayed
with us, although these days the kids take themselves off
upstairs for a bath before bedtime. When they were very tiny
I would usually get in the bath with them and I loved to watch
their little faces as they felt the warm water on their skin.
Later on, when they were a bit more robust, they both had a
little chair that helped them sit up in the bath by themselves.
This meant my hands were free for swishing and splashing
and pouring water over them, which made them both giggle
so much! I've got so many photos of them both beaming with
joy in the bath, all big smiles and dewy eyelashes.

Top tip

Avoid bathing your baby in the first few days after they arrive, until the separation of the umbilical cord is complete. Washing can disrupt the flora at the base of the cord and potentially hinder the natural process of cord separation. If you want to clean them, do a top-and-tail wash with warm water and cotton wool pads or reusable wipes. Or you can simply wait. It's up to you!

Rashes and Other Things That Worried Me

NAPPIES, WIND AND ALL THINGS WEE AND POOP

Chapter Four

I was Aunty Emma before
I was Mama; I've got an older
brother and a baby brother
and they both managed to
have children before me.

I always took my aunt-ly duties very seriously and changed
my nieces' and nephews' nappies when it was time. I figured
I had things pretty much sewn-up in that department. So
much so that I didn't really give it any thought at all before
I had my own babies with their own (super cute) bottoms
to change. I bought myself a funky nappy bag and set up a
change station on top of the chest of drawers in the bedroom.
We were good to go!

I didn't realise at that stage just how much of my time as
a new mum would be spent changing nappies. That my baby
would need up to eight nappy changes a day, sometimes more
if they were poorly (or had weed all over the new one just as

it was going on, as was often the case). Or that each change would generate a fistful of wipes and a nappy bag to dispose of, so that every week we'd produce an entire big black bin bag full of nappy waste alone. Or that often the contents of their nappies, especially in the early days, would seep out the top or the side of the nappy, and all over the beautiful white babygrows I liked to dress them in, so that each nappy change would also mean a babygrow change, and probably a vest change, and a deep wash and/or a soak in detergent. In short, I hadn't anticipated how many hours of my day would be devoted to the business of my baby's business.

Now that nappies quite literally are my business, with Kit & Kin, I'm astonished by how little I knew; about nappies and how they work, about what's in them and how to handle that side of caring for my baby. Because when you think about it, alongside feeding, changing nappies and processing all the associated waste and washing is probably the thing you spend most of your time as a new parent doing. And apart from us and our own skin, nappies are the things we put closest to our precious babies and their bottoms, for anything up to four years! And yet when I look back I realise I didn't know anything about them, other than the fact that I could choose between using disposables and washables.

When Beau was born, I was just becoming aware of the problems the world was facing around climate change. Like many of us, I knew I wanted to make changes and live a greener life. But being able to make those choices as a mum wasn't as easy as it is today. Eco or more ethical products were still kind of 'alternative' and they definitely weren't available on the shelf in the supermarket to pick up with your weekly

shop. You had to really know what you were looking for. I was a busy working Spice Girl, and as a family we were often on the road or away from home. Washables, as much as I liked the idea, just weren't going to work with our lifestyle.

So we used disposables. We were given some in the hospital (no one even asked us if we were going to be using anything else. I know many hospitals are now offering cloth nappies to mums and newborns instead and that is great!), and we continued to use that brand – one of the big names you see in chemists and the supermarkets – once we got home. And we used the same brand's wipes and nappy sacks. It was just one of those automatic, familiarity things, like the way you always buy the same brand of ketchup or baked beans.

So when Beau got nappy rash – red, sore spots and inflamed skin all over his bottom and the tops of his little chubb-a-chubb legs – I never really questioned why it was happening. It was just another accepted part of the process. I put it down to too much time with a nappy on, or maybe it was something I had eaten that had come through via breastfeeding to his wee or poop? I tried talcum powders, barrier creams, antiseptics and all sorts of products on his sore bits. But nothing really seemed to work, apart from not wearing a nappy.

So we had a lot of naked bum time, keeping him as nature intended, as much as we could. Who doesn't love their baby's bare bottom anyway? But we all got weed on a few times! In fact, Beau has probably weed on all of the Spice Girls at some point. But, like using washables, simply not wearing nappies and weeing on everyone wasn't a great fit with the life we were leading at that point. So more often than not, Beau was in a disposable nappy.

I wish I'd known then what I know now about nappies! We muddled through with Beau, but when Tate came along a few years later, I really began to understand what disposable nappies are made of. Tate had already had the problems with tongue-tie and feeding, so when rashes appeared on their skin I was more primed this time to investigate and find out what was causing the problems. It turned out that Tate had eczema as well as nappy rash and much of it was linked to a dairy intolerance (see page 169–73 for more on eczema and page 174 for dairy). But in the process of getting to the bottom (ahem) of their skin problems, I found out so much about disposable nappies.

Co-founder of Kit & Kin and expert in the production of nappies, Chris Money has all the information you need on this.

TAKE IT FROM THE EXPERT

CHRISTOPHER MONEY –
CO-FOUNDER OF KIT & KIN

THE SCIENCE OF DISPOSABLE NAPPIES

Most of the disposable nappies on the shelves in the supermarkets and high-street chemists, even though they can look and feel like a kind of tissue, are actually made from oil and plastic.

There's a liner, or topsheet, made of a plastic polymer called polypropylene, that sits right next to a baby's skin and 'wicks' away moisture into the absorbent pad in the middle. This core is made of SAP (super-absorbent polymer), little gel balls that can hold up to 40 times their own size and weight in liquid (why you get those big, heavy wet nappies). And then there's another layer of polypropylene on the outside that keeps it all in the nappy. That's three layers of different chemicals and plastics all pushed up against a baby's soft skin, and held in place with sticky tabs.

The ease and simplicity of disposable nappies is undeniable, and without them so many of us would be slaves to our laundry baskets, but it can be a bit of a shock to learn about what most disposable nappies are made of.'

NAPPY NUMBERS

<u>8 million:</u> number of disposable nappies going to landfill every day in the UK.

<u>200–500:</u> number of years it takes for a regular disposable nappy to decompose.

<u>2.5:</u> number of years the average child spends in nappies.

<u>6,000:</u> average number of disposable nappies used by a baby.

I had been so careful about what I fed my babies, the detergent I used to wash their clothes and the products I put on their skin. I wouldn't let anyone smoke near them, I didn't even like them being in their buggies by a busy road. And yet here I was wrapping their bottoms up in plastic and chemicals I'd never heard of.

The more I learnt about what's inside disposable nappies, and the more naked bum time we had, the more I began to realise that it wasn't the entirely natural wees and poops that were causing the nappy rash, it was the chemicals in the nappies and wipes themselves. It was the nappies, not their contents, that were causing nappy rash!

Just as bad was the discovery that in the UK alone we put 8 million disposable nappies into landfill every day. Every day! And because they are made of virgin oil and plastic, they don't break down in the land. Pretty much every disposable nappy that any of us has used is still in one piece, in landfill somewhere, along with the wipes and the nappy bags we wrapped them up in. How is that for a sobering thought? It just made me so sad, and is really what led to Kit & Kin's biodegradable nappies being created.

The solution: biodegradable disposables

They weren't around when Beau was small, but in recent years we've finally seen more earth-friendly, eco-nappies becoming available. These nappies have all the convenience of a regular disposable nappy, but are made with natural materials that break down more quickly over time and don't contain harsh chemicals that irritate babies' skin. For example, at Kit & Kin, we use plant-derived materials (from corn) in our nappies, that are all sustainably sourced and produced in carbon-neutral factories that don't pollute the environment. It's a lot easier to throw away a used disposable nappy when you know it's not going to be sitting in landfill for another 200 years! Plus all our nappies are approved by dermatologists and use super-gentle, plant-derived materials to keep irritants away from babies' skin.

What about washables?

Washables have come such a long way since my babies were small! Back then, using washables meant soaking dirty towels in buckets, boil-washing and sending your nappies off to laundry services. It all seemed so complicated and messy. And their bottoms always looked so huge! I always thought all that fabric between their legs would stop them being able to crawl.

Luckily for you mamas today, washables are virtually unrecognisable from the clumpy, complicated things they used to be. There's no getting around the fact that you do still need to wash them, but you don't have to soak or boil them, you can just chuck them in the washing machine. Today's reusable nappies are almost as simple as disposables to put on and take off. They're streamlined, with figure-hugging outers and super-slim inner layers. They have Velcro and poppers to keep them in place and that let them grow with your baby. (At Kit & Kin we've made our washables even greener, using hemp and other plant-based materials for softness and extra absorbency on the inner layer, and making the outer layers with reclaimed nylon fishing nets! If you really want to minimise the impact of your baby's nappies on the planet, it doesn't get much better.)

Washables are also a great way to save some cash! There's an upfront investment to think about, but over time you will definitely spend less on washables than disposables. On the flipside, you'll probably use more energy at home washing and drying, and of course you'll spend more of your physical time on laundry. You have to weigh up the pros and cons and work out what's best for your family.

Top tip

—

Every local authority has a different way of handling disposable nappy waste. Some are now tackling the problem with separation schemes that break up disposable nappies and clean and recycle the plastics in them. If you want to make the best choice for the environment, but aren't sure which nappy route to take, it's worth asking your local council for some information about how they are tackling the problem. They might also offer incentives and services such as kerbside collection of nappy waste or collecting washables for laundry. The Women's Environmental Network also has loads of helpful information and advice (see Useful Resources on page 246). Check it out!

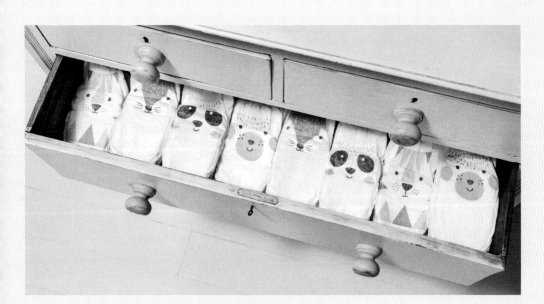

Mix it up!

I'm not here to tell you which nappies are best for you and your family. Disposables are so convenient and lightweight. Washables are less wasteful and cost less over time. Which route to take is something only you can decide on, but, like breastfeeding and bottle-feeding, one option is to try a bit of both. Experts reckon that even if you only use a washable nappy once a day throughout the time that your baby is in nappies, you'll put around 900 fewer nappies into landfill overall. And that has to be a good thing, right?

Experts say that if you only use a washable nappy once a day you'll put around 900 fewer nappies into landfill overall!

Top of the Poops

Your baby's poop can change colour quite a lot over the first few weeks and months, right up until you start introducing solids, and even then, certain foods can do strange things! Don't be alarmed if it looks a bit crazy in there – Marie Louise has a brilliant chart that you can use to check what the different do-do's mean:

TAKE IT FROM THE EXPERT

MARIE LOUISE, THE MODERN MIDWIFE – NHS MIDWIFE

 <u>First poops:</u> The very first poops your baby does are a blackish-green. This is the meconium from the amniotic fluid your baby was living on inside you. It doesn't look very nice, but don't worry, it will work its way out of their system usually by around day five. If your baby continues to pass meconium after day five it is important to let your midwife know.

Breastfed: Breastfed poops are liquid, with a mustardy-yellow colour and sometimes what looks like little seeds or grains in it. Breastfed poop smells kind of sweet (some parents even confess the smell of this poop is a guilty pleasure!).

Bottle-fed: Digesting formula works differently to breast milk and the poop of a bottle-fed baby is usually more solid as a result. It's still pale yellow or a yellowish brown colour, but with a smell that's more like grown-up poop.

Diarrhoea: Has the liquid consistency of breastfed poop, but not as aromatic! Can be yellow, green or brown and likes to leak out of your baby's nappy. Because it's so watery it can cause dehydration, so make sure you see a doctor immediately if it lasts for longer than 24 hours, or has blood in it.

Constipation: Little hard poops are often a sign of constipation. You might notice your baby straining extra hard when they are trying to do a poop! Make sure your baby is well-hydrated. A little blood can sometimes appear as a result of the straining, but if it continues make sure you see the doc.

Green poop: This can sometimes happen as your baby transitions from passing meconium to digested milk, or if your baby is breastfeeding but isn't getting as much of the full-fat milk from your boobs. It might be a latching on problem, or too much time between feeds. Talk to your health visitor or breastfeeding counsellor if this happens.

TOP TIP

You don't have to have a nappy bag. Sure, it's nice and handy to have a bag with special compartments for everything. Some come with folding change mats inside, which can be useful when you are out and about and need to do a quick change. But if you want to spend your money on other things, this is one purchase you really don't have to make if you don't want to. Just pop a nappy or two, a small packet of wipes, and something to lay your little one down on in your regular bag.

CHANGING PLACES: WHAT DO I NEED AND WHERE DO I DO IT?

When your baby is tiny it's nice to find somewhere quiet to change them if you can. You'll want to be extra gentle with them, especially while they still have a cord scab. Having a dedicated space for nappy changing gives you the opportunity to take as much time as you need and is usually a really lovely chance for some one-on-one smiles and gurgles.

CORD CARE

The stump from your new baby's umbilical cord usually takes a week or so to dry out and drop off. You don't need to do anything special with it, just try not to have anything too tight on or around it. You can roll down the top of their nappy so that it doesn't rub.

Have you ever heard of 'Lotus Birth'? This is a practice popular in southern Africa, Bali and parts of Australia, where the umbilical cord and placenta are left attached to your baby until the cord naturally falls off (anywhere between five and ten days). While it's still attached, the placenta is kept in a cloth and the cord is wrapped in a silk or cotton ribbon. Some mums say it's a great way of ensuring they get more rest in the early days, as they are less able to get up and out with their baby before this natural separation occurs. It would definitely make changing nappies more interesting!

You don't need a special baby changing table or unit (although you can get these) — you can use the top of a chest of drawers or a space on the floor. Just be extra careful as even though you think your baby can't go anywhere, accidents can happen. Never leave them unattended, even if it's just to turn away for a second. And always use a change mat with 'anti-roll' sides. ,

I had a lovely changing station all set up on top of the chest of drawers in the baby's room. It had plenty of room, space for a comfy change mat and a basket for wipes, bags and cream. And it was at a good height, which meant I wasn't bent over all the time. That was my special quiet place where I used to take them when they were very small.

But as time goes by, you'll probably find, like I did, that you become quite the expert at changing nappies and what used to take you ten or fifteen minutes is now over in two or three. I also found that I just didn't want to have to go all the way upstairs every time I changed them, or get up out of bed or off the sofa. So I often ended up changing them wherever I was. The bed or sofa was perfect because there was so much room and it was comfortable. I kept a little basket stocked with all the things I needed and made sure it was close by, and just did it like that, on the go.

Nappy basket: what you need

—

This is a really lovely, and easy, gift for new mums. I made one up for Geri and gave it to her at her baby shower and she loved it!

- a wipeable change mat
- nappies
- wipes and/or cotton wool
- nappy bags, if you are using them
- a natural cream or balm for rashes

Top tip

—

If your baby (like mine!) is a wriggler who wants to play at change time, I found that having a teether or a rattle handy was a great way to distract them, while you whip off their nappy and get the new one on! Changing them underneath a play arch is also a good way to keep them busy while you do a speedy change.

How to make your own wipes

One of my best mates, Jo, is a proper eco-warrior who makes her own amazing baby wipes. I love the idea of this, it's such a simple way to do your bit, there's no packaging and you know exactly what's in them. You don't have to use them all the time, you can still use regular wipes when you are out and about and just use these at home if you want to. She uses cut up pieces of fabric from the babygrows her kids have grown out of that are too far gone to hand down or pass on. We've all had a few of those!

Jo's natural wipes

Boil-wash a few old babygrows or T-shirts (jersey is best as it stays together and can stand some serious washing) that you don't mind cutting up. Then cut them into your wipe squares: 20cm x 20cm is a good size, but you can do any size you like! If you are a whizz at sewing and want a smarter look you can use the overlock stitch setting on your machine to finish the edges.

Pile them all up in a little basket or by the side of your change mat. Dampen with the natural solution (below) when it's time to wipe, and wash after use.

For the solution

1l water, boiled and cooled
700ml almond oil
2 tbsp natural body wash
3 tbsp pure aloe vera

• Pour all of the ingredients into a large jar and shake.

• Decant into an old hand soap pump or squeezy shampoo bottle, or similar.

• Use sparingly with your cloth wipes whenever you change a nappy.

What is nappy cream and which one should I use?

—

At Kit & Kin, Chris and I beleive that the best way to prevent nappy rash is to avoid using disposable nappies that contain chemicals. But even babies who wear eco-nappies or washables can sometimes get a rash (usually if they are unwell, or they have reacted to the detergent they are washed in), so it's a good idea to keep a nappy cream handy for when your little one gets sore. Many of the traditional so-called barrier creams that you find on the high street actually contain synthetic materials such as benzyl alcohol, that can irritate sensitive skin and make it drier and more sore. We would always recommend choosing a 100 per cent natural cream or balm (Kit & Kin Magic Salve is my favourite, but I'm biased!) that contains only natural oils and botanical extracts. Look especially for lavender and chamomile, as they are both brilliant at healing and restoring balance to your baby's delicate skin.

Skin to Skin

Marie Louise, aka The Modern Midwife, is an NHS midwife and a new mum, with a special interest in neonatal skin. Here she shares some of her best advice for looking after your baby's skin in the early weeks and months:

TAKE IT FROM THE EXPERT

MARIE LOUISE, THE MODERN
MIDWIFE – NHS MIDWIFE

NAPPIES

A nappy is on your baby's bottom pretty much 24/7, so it's good to bear in mind exactly what it is in such regular contact with. Many disposable nappies have chemicals, plastics, bleaches and preservatives in them. Biodegradable or washable nappies usually have none of these and tend to be kinder on the skin. (Environmental impact is less easy to define as it depends on waste management in your local area.) Do what you

'It takes newborns around four to six weeks to build up their own natural skin barriers so using wipes with synthetic chemicals in can strip these barriers and cause further irritation to their delicate skin.'

—

MARIE LOUISE, THE MODERN MIDWIFE

think is best for you and your family. It's fine to mix and match, try different nappies and see what you get on with best.

WIPES

It takes newborns around four to six weeks to build up their own natural skin barriers so using wipes with synthetic chemicals in can strip these barriers and cause further irritation to their delicate skin. The skin needs to be given the opportunity to mature and develop its impressive array of defence mechanisms. Avoid wipes that contain perfumes, alcohol, artificial colours, parabens or phthalates as these can cause further irritation to their delicate skin. Try to use cotton wool in boiled, cooled water in the early days if you can.

NAPPY RASH

Nappy rash is very common in babies, and most will get it at some point, but it will usually be fairly mild and self-resolving. Seeing red, raised or sore, broken skin can be upsetting and/or worrying for parents. Here are my top tips to help prevent and manage nappy rash:

- <u>Try to change your baby as soon as you realise they have a dirty nappy.</u> No mad rush, but keeping their sensitive skin clean and dry can prevent irritation.

- <u>A thin layer of nappy cream can help heal and protect the skin.</u> Opt for a natural and ideally organic barrier cream that doesn't contain preservatives, colours or perfumes.

- <u>Wash your hands before using nappy cream</u> because sometimes you can spread bacteria into products if your hands aren't clean.

- <u>After a bath or wash, make sure the skin is completely dry</u> before putting a fresh nappy on. Avoid talcum powder because inhalation can be harmful for your baby. Pat dry if you're pushed for time or, best of all, wait for the skin to dry naturally.

With a good nappy and skincare regime nappy rash should self-resolve. But if the rash persists, your baby is unwell or you have concerns over the severity of the rash always contact your GP.

TOP TIP

Babies are often more likely to develop a nappy rash if they are unwell, or teething. Why? Because they produce more saliva, which is swallowed down into their tummy, which can have an effect on the gut and lead to an increased need for nappy changes. If your baby is unwell or teething, their temperature may slightly rise and this can also have an effect on the gut — sometimes making nappy rash worse. As well as changing your baby regularly around these times, make sure you allow their skin to breathe and give as much nappy-free time as possible.

NAPPYNESS IS A STATE OF MIND

Have some nappy-free time! It is one of the best things for your baby's skin. Just pop some puppy pads or incontinence sheets down on the floor. Young babies love being naked and exploring their body. I often give my little one some clothes-free time and let her enjoy the freedom of being naked; even if she does try to eat her toes! Just make sure that the room is warm.

A WORD ABOUT NEWBORN SKIN

Newborn babies' skin is sensitive and delicate, and more at risk of damage than mature skin.

When they're born your baby experiences some really big physiological changes, as their skin adapts from life in your tummy, where it's warm and wet, to life outside, where it's around 15 degrees cooler and dry. But don't worry! <u>The human body is extraordinary and ever so clever. Although sensitive and vulnerable, your baby's skin knows exactly what to do.</u> All you need to do is support these adaptations and give their skin every opportunity to perform at its best.

Here's what you need to know about the science behind your new baby's beautiful skin:

ACID MANTLE

When born, your baby's skin surface is alkaline, with an average pH of 6.34. However, within days, the pH falls to about 4.95 (acidic) forming what's called the acid mantle, a fine film that rests on the surface of the skin and acts as a protective barrier that repels toxins and infections throughout their lifetime.

VERNIX CASEOSA (VC)

Also known as birthday frosting, VC is that white, cream cheese-like stuff your baby is covered in when they are born. Although it might look mucky, it is actually a highly sophisticated bio-film consisting of antimicrobial peptides, proteins and fatty acids. These combine to form a protective barrier that is not only antibacterial but also antifungal. Do not remove the birthday frosting! Leave it to be absorbed like a cream; it helps your baby to maintain an intact epidermal barrier.

SKINCARE FOR NEWBORNS

Use only water to wash your baby for at least the first four weeks, as this will allow all the natural processes to work. If you want to introduce soaps and washes after then, here are some important considerations:

- There is no need to bath a newborn daily; two or three times a week is adequate. Some parents choose not to bathe their baby at all for the first four weeks.

- Wash cloths and flannels can be quite harsh, try using your hands and organic cotton wool or a natural sponge instead.

- <u>Ears, nose and eyes should be left alone</u> and avoid using cotton buds.

- <u>VC should always be left to absorb naturally,</u> so avoid soaps and washes in the first few weeks.'

HYPOALLERGENIC, SAY WHAT?

You'll see lots of products describing themselves as 'hypoallergenic', but what does it really mean? The word simply means that it is relatively unlikely to cause an allergic reaction. However, it doesn't guarantee anything and often many of the basic ingredients used in the manufacture of hypoallergenic products are the same as for standard formulations. If you're at all worried about irritating your baby's skin, always check the ingredients and avoid words like phthalates, alcohols, colours and parabens.

'

Goodbye Nappy Rash, Hello Eczema!

I first noticed the little red rashes in the folds of Tate's elbows and behind their knees. Tate was about six months old and it was that lovely time in the morning when they had just woken up all smiles and gurgles and we were having a cuddle on the big bed in our room. The sunlight was streaming in through the curtains and I had been blowing raspberries on their tummy and playing 'peep-bo', hiding my face behind their upturned feet and making them shriek with laughter. As I held their legs I noticed the sore red patches in the crease behind the knees and then on the arms. I knew immediately it was eczema, as I'd had it myself when I was younger.

I was reminded how my children are both such different souls, inside and out. Beau's nappy rash wasn't nice for him, but we knew it would clear up given enough nappy-free time and the right products that didn't aggravate the skin. With Tate and eczema, we had a whole new set of skin problems to solve.

Like most mums would, I headed straight to the chemist and picked up all the creams that said they were for eczema, many of them familiar brands that had been in the bathroom cupboard when I was growing up. I smeared the thick, white creams on the patches and used the body wash in the bath, but they didn't seem to make any difference; in fact, they seemed to make it worse. More red patches appeared on the inside of Tate's hands, the soles of their feet and behind their ears.

The next stop was the doctor, who prescribed us what's called a topical corticosteroid cream. This is a really common, standard treatment for eczema, but something about it made me uncomfortable. Maybe it was just hearing the word 'steroid'; I didn't feel right putting that on my baby's skin. I couldn't help wondering if there was another way.

I looked up the side effects of the cream we'd been prescribed on the NHS website and it said that, although uncommon, it could cause symptoms like a change in skin colour, thinning of the skin and rosacea. Things were already bad enough, I didn't want to put something on my baby's body that might actively make it worse. So we took the decision not to use it and set about finding a different path, trying to find the cause and not just treat the symptoms.

Our initial thinking was that it must be the milk, so we tried various different formulas, all with varying levels of success. We learnt years later that Tate actually has a lactose intolerance (not a full-blown allergy, but their body definitely doesn't like cow's milk), but while at times it seemed to calm it down, even switching their milk to lactose-free formula didn't always keep the eczema at bay.

Next up was the detergent we washed all their clothes in. We tried all the different options – many of the high-street brands offer 'hypoallergenic' and sensitive skin products – but nothing seemed to make a difference.

It was only when we stopped using the bubble bath at bath time that I realised what had been causing the problems. Even though it promised it was gentle on baby's skin, and even though Beau didn't seem to be affected in the same way, whatever was in the wash and the bubble bath we'd been using was enraging Tate's skin.

Like with the nappies and the nappy cream, there are so many 'trusted' brands and products out there that are actually full of chemicals that can harm a baby's delicate skin. We'd been given various products as gifts or had picked things up that we liked the look of and never really thought about what was in them or that they might be harmful for a baby's skin. You just kind of trust all the promises on the packaging, don't you? But I realised I'd need to do some homework.

Once I stopped putting anything in their bath at wash time, though it didn't completely cure Tate's skin, my goodness it made a really noticeable and immediate difference.

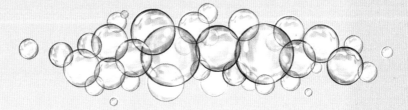

A word about eczema from Marie Louise, The Modern Midwife:

TAKE IT FROM THE EXPERT

MARIE LOUISE, THE MODERN
MIDWIFE – NHS MIDWIFE

> Here in the UK we have some of the world's
> highest rates of eczema or atopic dermatitis.
> Research shows that there has been a steady
> rise of this now common infant skin condition
> since the introduction of manufactured baby
> products (washes, wipes, disposable nappies,
> etc.) from the mid-twentieth century onwards.
>
> But in my experience as a midwife, skin
> conditions such as eczema are multifactorial —
> they can't always be traced to one cause. Diet,
> genetic heritage, domestic settings and even
> proximity to air pollution can all play their
> part. So I want to be clear and note that sometimes,
> no matter what a parent does to prevent it,
> their child may still develop eczema.

You can only do your best with the information and situation you are in. This is not the time to play the blame game or get a dose of good old mum guilt! The important thing is not to fly solo, and to seek help and support from your midwife, GP and other mums.

WHAT EXACTLY IS ECZEMA?

Eczema is a really common skin condition that makes skin itchy, dry and sore, becoming red on lighter skin, and darker brown, purple or grey on darker skin. Atopic eczema (atopic dermatitis) is the most common form of eczema, and tends to affect children under one more than any other age group, although you can develop it as an adult too. It can appear anywhere on the body, but usually affects the hands, elbows, backs of knees and the face and scalp.

There is no one cause of eczema, but it does seem to happen to people who have allergies and intolerances, and people who have asthma and hay fever. Other factors like the chemicals in soaps, the weather and stress can also seem to trigger it. It's not something that can be entirely cured, but it can usually be managed and may even clear up by itself as a baby grows up. Always talk to your doctor if you have any concerns about eczema.

DAIRY INTOLERANCE
OR MILK ALLERGY?

Dairy or lactose intolerance is relatively
common, and can be more common in people
of African, Caribbean or Asian heritage.
It's different from a full-blown milk
or dairy allergy in that most people
with lactose intolerance can consume
small amounts of lactose (the sugar
found in cow's milk) without experiencing
serious problems. An allergy is an immune
system reaction and even the slightest
particle of dairy could set off wheezing,
coughing and rashes. If you think your
baby has a lactose intolerance or you
are worried about allergies, talk to
your doctor or health visitor. It's best
not to diagnose these things yourself
as any kind of dietary restriction
can cause complications. Your GP will
be able to refer you to a specialist
dietician if necessary.

Rashes and Other Things That Worried Me

It's Playtime!

UNDERSTANDING DEVELOPMENT
AND FORGETTING
COMPETITIVE MILESTONES

Chapter Five

I was astonished to learn
that in the first year of life
a baby's brain will double
in weight!

Your baby is born with all the neurons they need and spends the first year busily making connections in their brain that fuel a growing sense of awareness of the world around them. As they begin to see and hear and understand the world, they'll start to sleep less and want to be around you more, joining in all the fun!

I absolutely loved watching both of my babies going through this growth – it was a kind of awakening I guess. Coming out of the very early weeks when they seemed to sleep so much and into the third, fourth and fifth months, so much was going on for them and every day there was a new development: a smile, a word, a movement. It was all so exciting!

I'd seen what I thought was a smile on Beau's face plenty of times before. But people always tell you it's wind when they are tiny or a 'reflex smile' (basically an involuntary smile), so I'd never been sure if it was real. But I'll always remember Beau's first real smile. We'd rented a house in LA for the pre-tour training.

It was comfortable and close to the studios where I needed to be for training and rehearsals. Best of all, it had a beautiful garden where Jade and I could relax with Beau, who was now three months old, whenever we got some downtime.

Beau had woken up from a nap all bright-eyed and raring to go, and Jade had brought him out into the garden. The sun was out, but it was that lovely late afternoon warmth rather than the blazing heat you get earlier in the day, and as soon as Jade passed Beau to me in the sunshine, he just beamed. I knew it was a real smile this time, it was in his eyes.

I couldn't help welling up in that moment – the pure joy of feeling that connection with him was just overwhelming and so lovely. I know it will be for you too, mama, when the moment comes. It was also the beginning of a new phase in the care and keeping of Beau, where at last it felt like I was getting some good feedback! Until then it had mostly been a case of deciphering what his crying meant: was it feeding, changing or sleeping? Now he could smile, it felt like a whole new dimension of fun and simple pleasure had opened up. Things were getting interesting!

Beau in the garden in LA

It's Playtime!

179

All smiles

—

Your baby's reflex smile will happen until around two months old, and the first real one will happen somewhere between one-and-a-half and three months. Reflex smiles tend to be shorter and can happen at random times. Real smiles happen in response to something, like seeing your face or hearing daddy's voice.

As the smiles and chuckles began to come in thick and fast, so it seemed like Beau's curiosity had been awakened. Suddenly, he was interested in so much; whether it was watching me eat or looking at the way his own hands moved, he had this look of total amazement on his face at times that really made me laugh.

He was growing stronger, too. It would be a good few months until he could really hold his head up properly, but his coordination and the strength in his arms and shoulders grew so that, as he learnt to smile more, he was also able to move his head around and see who was talking or what was making a noise. This was especially funny when he was feeding as sometimes he'd be right in the middle of a bottle and hear something – maybe it was Phoebe the dog barking or the sound of Jade talking – and he'd be visibly torn between wanting

It's Playtime!

to carry on with his milk and turning round to see what the noise was. He'd have a quick look and then a quick suck; the sight of him trying to do both at once was so funny!

This was such a lovely time, now I look back on it. He wasn't yet able to walk, so I still had a lot of cuddles and closeness, but at the same time he was more robust and I didn't feel so worried all the time. I carried him around with me on my hip, a position most babies seem to love as they can see everything that's going on and be at face height with you. I loved it too, but obviously as they get bigger it's a strain on the back, especially if they are at that pre-walking wriggler stage! There are some great slings and hip seat carriers around now that can help as they get bigger.

I still had a lot of cuddles and closeness, but at the same time he was more robust and I didn't feel so worried all the time.

What's Best for Carrying Your Baby?

Julia Minchin is the designer of the award-winning Hippychick Hipseat, so she knows her slings from her carriers. Here she gives her advice on how to pick the right one for you:

TAKE IT FROM THE EXPERT

JULIA MINCHIN – DESIGNER OF AN AWARD-WINNING BABY CARRIER

❛ Baby carriers are brilliantly practical and can really help you connect with your baby. Having your baby right up close to you will enable you to recognise particular signals and maintain all that lovely communication between you both. They are marvellously convenient for travelling on planes, trains and automobiles — and going anywhere with the baby that the buggy won't, or can't, go.

There are so many baby carriers to choose
from: slings, soft strap-ons and framed back
carriers. When choosing your baby carrier,
remember that you're important too! Choose
something you feel comfortable wearing.

- Go to a specialist baby wearing group or baby
  sling library to try out different styles
  and see what works best for you. Some of the
  stretchy wraps can be incredibly difficult to
  figure out how to use and they'll be able to
  take you through the process, step by step.

- If buying from a shop, do read the
  instructions or watch a video online
  for the type you have chosen! An improperly
  positioned carrier may be unsafe for your
  baby and could give you back issues,
  especially if you are wearing them for
  extended periods.

- A well-fitting carrier will help to take
  the strain off your body and ensure that
  you don't end up with long-term back pain.

- Always check the washing instructions.
  Ideally you want the material to be machine
  washable and shrink-proof.

- If you have twins, there are slings
  available that enable you to carry two

babies safely, but ask your midwife or visit
a baby carrying group for the best advice on
design to suit you and your babies.

- <u>Baby carriers</u> needn't only be for outdoors.
  You can, and should, be able to wear your
  baby carrier around the house. But do also
  give your baby plenty of time out of the
  carrier to stretch out and have a kick
  or crawl around and discover the world
  around them.

- <u>From six months of age up to two and half,</u>
  you may wish to opt for a hip seat carrier.
  Many parents pick up a baby and prop them
  on their hip, which throws the whole body

out of alignment and can cause back pain. A hip seat carrier is a belt that wraps around the waist, supporting your lower back and is extremely comfortable to wear. There's a seat on one side where your baby or toddler can perch comfortably and naturally.

- <u>A hip seat carrier can also be an ideal solution</u> for babies and toddlers with hip dysplasia as the perch is ideally shaped for the comfortable and natural positioning of the plaster casts, but always get the advice of a medical professional as individual cases vary.

<u>Be sensible!</u> Don't carry your baby in a carrier while doing anything that may harm them, such as cooking, jogging or any kind of sport. And never wear your baby in a car. Always use a car seat suitable for their age and weight.'

TOP TIP

'Though there have been limited studies on the subject, research has suggested that babies tend to cry less when carried. So if you're looking for ways to reduce crying, baby wearing might just be worth a go.'

HAVE YOU HEARD OF ATTACHMENT THEORY?

The theory that staying close to a mother or father, or other significant caregiver, can actually benefit a baby's physical and emotional development was developed by British psychoanalyst John Bowlby in the thirties. Bowlby studied how children in care, who had been separated from their mothers or caregivers at a young age, were affected in later life (general gist: not so great) and his resulting 'attachment theory' laid the foundations for the way we approach parenting today. Later on in the sixties, American paediatrician William Sears took it a step further with his 'attachment parenting' philosophy, suggesting that babies need to be physically held and maintain bodily closeness with a parent pretty much continuously in order to thrive. It seems quite normal nowadays to wear your baby in a sling or a carrier, but fewer than 100 years ago people were still leaving babies outside in their prams all day and thought that picking them up if they cried would 'spoil' them! If you're interested in family psychology and want to find out more about it, search online for 'attachment theory' and 'attachment parenting'. It's fascinating stuff!

Music and Laughter

Tate's big stimulus was always music. It won't surprise you to know that music has always been a huge part of life for my family. We are literally always singing in our house, and there is rarely a moment when music isn't playing. (We both love all sorts of stuff, but there's a place in both our hearts for all the Motown tunes. It was quite a special moment in 2019 when we recorded 'You're All I Need to Get By' together for my album, *My Happy Place*.)

With Tate's acid reflux and tongue-tie, they'd had a difficult start and been, understandably, a bit grumpy in the early months. Music was our salvation. We played classical music to Tate when they were in my tummy and carried on with that at bedtime and change times – it always  brought a little smile out for us even when things were really uncomfortable for Tate. And if we weren't playing tunes we were singing nursery rhymes and lullabies like 'Incy Wincy Spider', 'Old MacDonald' and, my favourite, 'Clap, Clap, Handies'.

Singing and music are such an instinctive part of being a mama. Whether it's to soothe them or just to delight them, singing to our babies and playing music, moving to the sounds, just seems to come so naturally, and bring so much joy. And goodness we all need that, don't we?

So if you are ever feeling low and tired, or like being a mama is all work and no play, put on some music and dance with your baby or sing them a song. I guarantee everyone will feel so much better!

As they got older, both of my babies loved to lie on a play mat, under a baby gym. We had a jungle-themed one, with a little bell and a mirror and some crackle fabric that they tugged at and wiggled and kicked. Later, as they grew stronger in their arms and neck, they rolled over and looked at the patterns on the mat and tried to grasp toys we put there. But looking back, I remember that the thing the pair of them loved the most was lying on our landing and looking up at the beams in the ceiling! We have big old black beams across a white ceiling up there. Especially when they were tiny, both of them seemed to be mesmerised by the lines they made.

It won't surprise you to know that music has always been a huge part of life for my family.

I absolutely loved it when my babies started to make sounds and noises, particularly when they had a very serious expression on their face while basically blowing raspberries at me. You could see and hear how much they wanted to join the conversation, and often seemed to think that they were genuinely having a chat with us!

I think they were both around six months old when they really started to gurgle and babble, and both seemed to be imitating the sounds Jade and I made. (It was a little after his first birthday when Beau said his first word: 'apple'. I'll never forget it because he had terrible croup and while he was poorly I called 111. The person on the phone asked me to describe his cough and the only thing that I could think of was that it sounded like Jimmy Carr's laugh!).

The Science of Music and Rhythm

Like so much of this baby business, it turns out that there's a reason why music is so important. Mother Nature knows best, and she definitely knows her way around a beat. Rhythm and movement aren't only great fun for babies, they lay the foundations for all sorts of important things like speech, language, movement and coordination.

Here, leading child psychologist (and dad) Dr Sam Wass, from Channel 4's *The Secret Life of…* series, explains how and why music and rhythm is so important for young babies:

TAKE IT FROM THE EXPERT

DR SAM WASS – CHILD
PSYCHOLOGIST

' So much of a baby's early development is about
rhythm! From the moment they are born you
and your baby are engaged in a kind of dance,
adapting your rhythms to match one another.
Your baby learns their sense of self-control
by adapting their own, more chaotic, rhythms

(think of a baby kicking their legs in the cot, for example) to your adult rhythms, which are naturally more stable and controlled.

And we know that babies are very sensitive to music. Even from a young age (five months), babies can dance and time their movements in time with the beat, and even move faster when fast-paced music is playing. <u>Moving and listening to music together with your baby has also been shown to promote feelings of affiliation and trust (a bit like going clubbing with your friends)</u>.

Other research shows that — particularly in babies who have tough early life experiences, such as babies born prematurely — slow-paced music, such as lullabies, are effective both at helping infants to stay calm and in reducing anxiety in the parent.

Music is also about phrasing and pitch. Early on, babies only use their voices to attract your attention when they're unhappy. But over time, through matching their own vocalisations to yours, they learn how to use their voices to communicate emotions — first through musical ideas like pitch and repetitive rhythms, and then, eventually, through words.

THE EYES HAVE IT

Babies are heavily short-sighted at birth —
they can only see clearly up to a distance of
about 20cm — and see mostly in black and white.
Although research studies have shown that,
even within a couple of hours after birth,
babies prefer to look at faces and can recognise
their parents' faces and voices, most parents'
experience of the first few months after birth
is pretty thankless. Because they can't control
what they pay attention to, a young baby's eyes
can cross right over your face without appearing
to notice it at all — and they don't tend to
return a smile until around three months.

This doesn't mean that you shouldn't keep
trying, though. The more you can make your
face 'easy' for a baby to make sense of, the
faster they will learn to understand how to
'see' it — to find where the important features
are (your eyes, your mouth) and to recognise
emotions. So it's worth giving them a lot of
direct face-to-face time. And to make your
face as easy as possible for your baby to
understand, it's worth holding your face still
(not moving), facing directly towards your
baby and positioning yourself against a plain
bright background — so it's easier for your
baby to tell where your face stops and the
background starts.

CALL AND RESPONSE

Another feature of early development is how you respond to your child. A lot of babies' early movements are quite random — they'll suddenly, unpredictably, do something that looks like a smile, or a grimace, or make a noise. And research suggests that if you reliably copy your baby's random movements back to them, it could help them to become more aware of what they're doing, which is essential in helping them gain control.

The same is true for vocalisations and learning language. A lot of babies' early noises are random, but if you copy back to them what they do, then even from an early age they respond. This can lead to turn-taking — call and response — which helps them gain self-control and awareness of what the noises that they're making sound like to other people. Some famous early research into parent–child vocal interactions actually used musical notation to write this down: baby makes a noise, and parent responds and elaborates on it a bit, and then they respond back. These are the early origins of all forms of music.

Emotions

You can also use this pattern of call and response to help your baby to understand and control their emotions. Again, a lot of emotional fluctuations in young babies are pretty random — if you look at how their heartbeats change when they go suddenly from very calm, to very excited, and back again. When a baby is worked up, picking them up and moving around the room, or walking them up and down the stairs, can help because it brings your heart rate up to a level which is closer to theirs — so you're matching your state to theirs. And then, when your baby's heartbeat is synchronised to yours, as you calm back down again, this will help your baby to calm down, too.

Toys, Toys, Everywhere

Between Jade and I we have literally hundreds of relatives and what with all the Spice Girls for aunties and all our friends, we were very fortunate to have lots of gifts for them both when they were born. We had rattles, mobiles, teddies, and banana teethers galore.

But sometimes it was the simplest things – like those beams on the landing or the light reflecting off a disco ball in the living room – that seemed to captivate them far more than the beautiful soft toys they had. They both loved playing peek-a-boo and would squeal with delight when I hid my face behind a towel while they were in the bath. It was the interactions between us that they loved more than anything.

Toys to Support Your Baby's Development

Alexis Ralphs is a father of four and a former nursery teacher who founded One Hundred Toys, a company whose ethos is 'fewer, better toys'. Here he gives his advice on which toys can help support your baby's growing curiosity:

TAKE IT FROM THE EXPERT

ALEXIS RALPHS - FOUNDER OF ONE HUNDRED TOYS

' All babies develop at different times and in different ways. For some, the physical milestones — sitting up, grasping objects, walking — come early, while for others they seem to take forever. Some babies enjoy the razzle-dazzle of a brightly coloured mobile from day one, while others seem only to want cuddles and calm. Whatever their preferences and needs, the good news is that all your baby really needs in the first few months of life is you. The model and appetite for exploration,

Mama You Got This

discovery and skills that you establish
with them now, have a long-lasting
impact on their emotional intelligence
and academic success 'in later life. And <u>the
good news is you already have everything you
need, because you are your child's first toy!</u>

In fact, two of the most natural responses
we have as parents in those early weeks and
months — singing nursery rhymes and rocking
our babies to sleep — are already working hard
on your behalf to give them a brilliant start.
Nursery rhymes are a great introduction to
literacy because they teach your baby early
phonic skills, the hearing and manipulating
of letter sounds, long before they can talk.

Meanwhile, and as unlikely as it sounds,
when you rock your baby in your arms or bounce
them gently in a chair you help them develop an
early sense of balance. You also challenge their
eyes to stay focused despite the movement — a
useful skill years later when they follow words
across a page as they learn to read. Cool hey?

If you do want to give them toys, or relatives
want to give them something, try to choose
toys that stimulate and engage their
developing physical skills, and ideally
open-ended toys that can grow with them.

'Nursery rhymes are a great introduction to literacy because they teach your baby early phonic skills, the hearing and manipulating of letter sounds, long before they can talk.'

—

ALEXIS RALPHS

My top toys for babies under 12 months are:

- <u>A baby gym,</u> with toys suspended from the arch, gives young babies who can't yet move something interesting to look at, especially if you need to pop out of the room or keep them occupied. As they begin to develop greater control over their limbs and coordination, a baby gym gives them something to grasp for. Look for one that can be adjusted as your baby grows and that gives you scope to change the toys, otherwise they get bored of seeing the same things all the time. Try hanging mirrors, crystals, natural sponges and other things with interesting textures or that might catch the light.

- <u>A high-contrast mobile</u> helps babies' perceptual development and focus. Newborns have poor eyesight, so while it might not be the prettiest mobile around, choose one with bold black-and-white shapes and patterns that will help your baby's eyesight develop.

It's Playtime!

- A playmat is a soft, safe space to put your baby down and let them explore their growing physicality. They'll lie on their backs at first and learn to turn their heads left and right. Regular tummy time helps them develop strength in their neck and back. Placing interesting toys just out of their reach encourages them to wriggle and stretch — all good practice for when they eventually start crawling.

- A rattle — the quintessential baby toy! Newborns' eyesight isn't well coordinated with their hearing so shaking a rattle for them helps them learn to track sounds. Later on a rattle makes a great grasping toy to help their developing strength and coordination. Choose a wooden one that feels warm and natural in their hands.

- A high-contrast book is a way to share time and focus with your baby, even though they can't read yet! Like the mobile, it's best to go for bold black-and-white images for now. Detailed pictures and pretty colours can come later.

- A soft toy or comforter can reassure your baby when you need to leave them or they can't see you. Soft toys with happy, smiling faces can be your child's first experience of friendship and companionship. Just don't lose it!

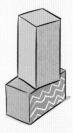

- <u>A ball</u>, preferably one that is soft and
  has bells inside, helps develop hand—eye
  coordination. Passing one back and forth
  with your baby is a lovely way to share
  a simple game together.

- <u>A walker</u> comes into its own as your baby
  learns to stand and pull themselves up.
  Rather than a plastic one with flashing
  lights on the front, choose something they
  can load up with blocks and other toys,
  then it can become part of their imaginative
  play as they grow older.

- <u>Wooden blocks</u> are among the most important
  toys you can invest in for your baby.
  At this stage they will just enjoy picking
  them up and hearing the sounds they make
  as they tumble down. Later on they will
  learn to build with them, and then to use
  them in their imaginative play.

'

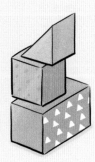

Checking in with Mama

SELF-CARE, WHY IT'S IMPORTANT AND HOW TO DO IT

Chapter Six

Self-care wasn't really a thing when my babies were small.

Sure, we knew about massages and pedicures, but we called that pampering! It was a spa day or a beauty treatment of some sort, and it was a treat, something you had for your birthday or a hen do. The idea that consciously taking time to care for and nourish yourself is necessary, even essential, has only really become mainstream in the last decade or so.

And I am so glad it has! Looking after yourself when you are a mama is so important. And I don't only mean taking care of your body and staying strong, although of course that is kind of crucial. I mean taking care of your entire well-being – physically and emotionally. Here in the UK, we have some of the highest rates of maternal postnatal depression in the world.

We struggle, we are tired and anxious and emotional, pulled in every direction, and juggling trying to keep everything together. Us mamas need to stop giving ourselves a hard time and start to look after ourselves too.

Knowing when to ask for help
—

Everyone finds being a new mama tough at times – it is such a big responsibility. Then there's the lack of sleep, the strain on your relationships, hormonal imbalance, time of year... Throw in climate change and all the other things we are all worrying about, and it can feel overwhelming.

I can't tell you exactly what's wrong or how to fix it. But I do know you can get help. Because there's a difference between feeling a bit fed up and stressed, and more serious things like anxiety and depression. If you feel you are struggling more than usual, it might be worth talking to your doctor or a friend about it. Pretending everything is all right can make things worse, and no one wants you to feel like that, mama.

There is so much help out there, and the stigma around mental health has really been lifted as more women speak out about their experiences. So you needn't ever feel embarrassed to talk about it. Feeling low is part of what makes you human!

Remember! Dads and partners can struggle too and sometimes might find it harder to ask for help. Encourage your partner to talk or get some help if you think they're struggling.

I've grown up with my mum giving me reflexology and reiki and all sorts of therapies, so I guess I've taken some aspects of self-care for granted. But even with my mum around, I know I neglected my own needs when the babies were small. I was so busy trying to do it all that I forgot to stop occasionally and fill up my own tank; from the big stuff I've talked about in this book, like pushing myself too hard on the stage and in my work, to little things like overdoing it on the caffeine and getting through endless cans of dry shampoo because I didn't have time to wash my hair. I was so worried about being a 'good' mum, and being seen to be that good mum, about proving to everyone that I could do it. It's crazy, when you think about it.

Mummy Bunton's guide to healing crystals

My mum is such a natural healer. She looks after everyone! When I presented the breakfast show on Heart FM she was like the show's mum – the whole team knew her and she'd often call in for a chat when we were on air. People still ask me, 'How is Mummy Bunton?'

Mummy Bunton has always been a spiritual person and used the power of crystal energy to heal and help with all kinds of problems, from anxiety and stress to creativity and even relationships. She gave all us Spice Girls crystals. I know Victoria won't mind me telling you that she gave Victoria one of her first crystals – an amethyst. I've worn a small rose quartz crystal in my bra for years, and I always keep a large amethyst crystal in my living room.

The idea is that crystals give off energy that promotes physical and emotional well-being. By reaching out for the crystals you want, they might just be able to help you reconnect with yourself and focus your mindset, which is a bonus when you are an anxious, overwrought new mama like I was.

But how do you know which crystals to choose and how to use them? Mummy Bunton is here to tell you:

A Quick Guide to Crystals from Mummy Bunton

❝ Choosing crystals is highly personal and will depend on the issues you are facing and the areas of your life that you need help with. For new mamas who are feeling exhausted, carrying a crystal or holding one just for a short while every day, gives you a little moment to centre yourself and come back to what is important amid all the chaos. Emma always goes for a rose quartz crystal as it's all about love and acceptance, whereas my favourite is white quartz; it brings clarity and concentration, and amplifies the energy of other crystals. You'll probably know which crystal is right for you simply by looking at it.

Here's a quick guide to what some of the most popular crystals can help with:

- **Hematite** helps you stay grounded in new situations and make the right decisions.

- **Selenite** helps to soothe and clear an overwhelmed mind.

- **Celestite** is a dreamy stone that promotes restfulness and sleep (a great anxiety-buster!).

- **Amethyst** is said to bring peace and harmony to the home.

- **Rose quartz** (Emma's favourite) is the stone of unconditional love, making it perfect for new mamas.

- **Angelite** brings a soothing energy to help with life transitions (great if you are moving house!).

- **Rhodonite** is known as 'the rescue stone' and helps remind you to stay calm, cool and collected.

Top tip

—

You don't need enormous crystals – a necklace, bracelet or anklet will work just as well and you can keep it on you all the time. Even holding a small crystal will touch the pressure points in your fingertips and help release stress. ,

Me and mummy Bunton

I'm not suggesting everyone needs to rush out and buy crystals though! Self-care can mean so many different things to different people. To me, self-care means anything that makes you feel better – it could be something as simple as listening to a podcast, taking a long hot bath, or just eating an entire box of chocolates. Whatever it is that means you are giving yourself some attention and don't feel you are running on empty – that's the real meaning of self-care.

To me, self-care means anything that makes you feel better – it could be something as simple as listening to a podcast, taking a long hot bath, or just eating an entire box of chocolates.

Walk on

For me, when the babies were little, self-care often meant taking a walk. I'm lucky to live near woodlands and being able to close the door behind me and step out with the dogs, even just for 20 minutes, seemed to always make everything feel better. (Although sometimes, if I was taking the baby with me, just getting out of the house seemed to take longer than the actual walk.)

You don't need me to explain the health benefits of exercise and fresh air, but when you have a small baby, it can be really difficult to get enough of both. Walking is such a simple, accessible way to put some exercise in your day. You can take the baby with you in the buggy or sling, or if someone can watch them for you, it's a quick, free and easy way to get your body moving, without having to get changed or go to a class or do anything else that takes up valuable time and money.

And walking doesn't have to mean heading out into the countryside. Walking in the city or town is just as beneficial and there are loads of great apps and websites now, with inner-city walking routes and trails for buggies and all sorts.

These days, my favourite self-care trick is simply taking a bath. I love my baths, and everyone in the family knows that if I'm having a bath I need at least half an hour in there without being disturbed. It's such a basic, simple thing, but to be able to take the time to wash and clean yourself is really quite a luxury when you think about it. And it's not only the physical act of getting clean, there's something emotionally rejuvenating about washing away the day and all its stresses and strains. I like lots of bubbles (I use Kit & Kin bubble bath of course! People often ask me if I really use the products and the answer is YES! I really do! They are so soft and gentle – we all use them. Even on Jojo the dog).

And while self-care can sound kind of selfish – all that time devoted to yourself goes against what we mamas have been taught to do – I've learnt that it is also about other people, and the people you spend time with. Self-care doesn't need to mean spending time alone, it can just mean surrounding yourself with the right people.

I have been so fortunate to be on this journey with Jade. Don't get me wrong, we have our differences like all couples do. He's such a perfectionist and I'm definitely not! We were always falling out over washing the babies' bottles. My washing up was never good enough – it still isn't! But I know that I am lucky to have found someone who has supported me all the way through this, even when it wasn't much fun for him.

Jade's top tips for being a perfect partner

—

I actually felt a little bit left out when both our babies were born! There was such a massive connection between them and Emma, I found myself secretly wondering when it would be my turn. I made sure I had plenty of skin-to-skin contact with them both as soon as they arrived and always had lots of cuddles and changed them, and did as much as I could, but really I knew this was a special time for Emma and that I needed to be patient – I would have my moment eventually.

In the meantime I just made sure I was available and, more importantly, prepared. I didn't want to be that guy waiting for my instructions. I made it my business to read all the books and do all the learning I could, so that when something happened, like a rash or they were sick, I knew how to handle it. Emma was really surprised once when Beau had a rash and I got a glass out to see if it disappeared under the glass. I'd read about this as a test for meningitis. Thankfully it did vanish under the glass and we were able to worry a little less as a result. I knew how emotional and nervous she was feeling at times, so I tried to make sure that if she got in a panic about something, I could be the reassurance that she needed.

Some other things you can do to help
a new mum:

- **Bring her a glass of water** when she's
  feeding the baby. Staying hydrated is
  vital!

- **Up your game in the kitchen** – cook the tea, keep
  everyone well-nourished, and clean up afterwards.

- **Remember, the simple things make a big difference.**
  A glass of wine, a cup of tea, fresh sheets on the bed...
  it all means you are looking after her.

- **Let her sleep when you can.** However tired you think
  you are, she is more tired than you. Never forget this!

- **Be patient daddy**, and know your time will come.

Reach out

Sometimes the people you least expect can become the
greatest allies when you really need them. The important
thing is that you have someone; whether it's a partner, an old
friend or a new one you've only just made, try to find someone
who has your back. New motherhood can be so isolating, but
you don't need to fly solo. A friend in need really is a friend
indeed, so never be afraid to reach out and ask for help.

Friendship never ends

I was the fourth Spice Girl to have children so I had loads
of support and advice from the girls when the time came.
We now have 12 children between us. Watching them grow
up, having their own amazing personalities, and all very much
like their mamas, makes me feel so proud of them. I am lucky
to have such a big, extended family. In fact, on our last tour, we
had a dedicated family room, where they all hung out together
while we were on stage – a bit of a change from the tattoo artists
and nightclubs that were a regular feature of our 1998 tour!

It's funny how becoming a mama can change things
between friends and sometimes the people you thought were
your besties for life can suddenly feel so far away if one of you
has children and the other doesn't. This definitely happened
with some of my close (non-Spice Girl) friends. I'd hear about
them getting together and going out to parties and get proper
FOMO. New babies can take over your life (as you are probably
realising right now!) and, before you know it, you haven't called
someone you really should have for months, and when you do
you have nothing to talk about except babies and how tired you
are. It can be hard to navigate these times, but knowing that
this is normal and something we all experience can help.

As can cutting yourself some slack. It has been my
experience that the friendships that really matter can weather
fallow periods; the friend who didn't have kids when you did
eventually has them and calls to ask your advice and finally
you can be there for her, or vice versa. And meanwhile you
will probably find that you meet one or two new friends

through having your baby, whether it's at a class or just being out and about. I was extremely lucky to be pregnant at the same time as one of my closest friends and going through everything at the same time as her was such a brilliant support and felt so natural. For all the love and support I got from Jade and my family, being able to have those very female conversations, whether it was about finding a good maternity bra, or sex, or feeling down, or whatever it was, with someone who was experiencing all these things at the same time, was a real support for me. I've got so many photos of our babies sitting together on the sofa or the pair of us feeding at the same time! I know it's not possible for everyone, we live such splintered lives now and many of us live miles away from our dearest friends, but if you can, find another mama to walk with you on this amazing journey.

If you can, find another mama to walk with you on this amazing journey.

The Importance of Self-Care

Doula Beccy Hands and midwife Alexis Stickland from The Mother Box specialise in looking after new mums and have lots of great advice for finding your 'tribe', among other things. Here they explain why self-care is important and how it's about so much more than candles and massages (although those are always nice, obviously!):

TAKE IT FROM THE EXPERT

BECCY HANDS & ALEXIS STICKLAND - DOULA AND MIDWIFE FROM THE MOTHER BOX

6 Did you know that in many non-Western cultures around the world, new mothers are encouraged to spend their first postnatal weeks and months devoted entirely to resting, feeding (themselves and their baby) and bonding with their baby? In Morocco, for example, a new mum gets taken to the hammam (a kind of spa/ steam bath), where her midwife steams her and gives her a salt scrub, washes her hair, sings

'Did you know that in many non-Western cultures around the world, new mothers are encouraged to spend their first postnatal weeks and months devoted entirely to resting, feeding (themselves and their baby) and bonding with their baby?'

—

BECCY HANDS AND
ALEXIS STICKLAND

to her, tells her stories and then swaddles her in a gorgeous cloth while she rests! She is relieved of all household chores and fed restorative meals by her community. She is encouraged to take as much time as she needs to heal properly, so she can restore her energy and focus on caring for her baby.

When we don't live in close communities or with extended family nearby, it's more difficult to take time to rest and heal. So many of us end up parenting in isolation. The West has a really high number of mums suffering with postnatal depression and anxiety, compared to cultures where mothers are nurtured and held, with care and company in their early mothering. We can't pour from an empty cup. And if we are depleted and sleep-deprived, we can't give our best to our babies. This is why it's important to remember that self-care isn't a luxury or an indulgence, it's an absolute necessity.

We know it's not always easy to find time for yourself when you've got a small baby around, so here are some suggestions for nurturing and simple self-care practices for every stage of your postnatal year. And remember, your postnatal body will take time to heal. Take the time you need, there is no rush — it is not a race to be the first back in your skinny jeans!'

SOOTHING YOUR SORE BITS

Vaginas, bottoms and boobs can all feel a bit tender after birth. Even C-section mums can be tender from pre-op pushing, piles and hormonal changes. You don't need expensive creams or medicines. Try making these easy herbal cooling pads at home:

1. Put three chamomile tea bags in a big jug, cover with boiling water and leave to steep for 30 minutes.

2. Place some maternity pads (the big bulky ones) and/or breast pads on a baking sheet, making sure the part of the pad that touches the skin is facing up.

3. Pour the tea over the pads, ensuring each one is fully soaked, then place the pads in the fridge for at least two hours to chill.

For sore vulvas and perineums: pop a pad in your pants and sit on it for ten minutes.

For sore bottoms/piles: push between the cheeks a little.

For sore nipples and breasts: place a chilled breast pad into your bra to sit against the nipple for ten minutes after each feed, or until the pain reduces.

TOP TIP

Many local authorities no offer self-
referral (i.e. you don't need to see the
doctor) for talking therapies like CBT
and counselling. NHS.uk or Mind.org.uk
both have lots of helpful information.

STAYING REGULAR

However your baby arrived, you will want to avoid
straining on the loo! Straining puts pressure
on your abdominal wall and perineum, and can
irritate any haemorrhoids. Staying well-hydrated
is key, especially if you are breastfeeding, and
will help you avoid becoming constipated. This
fabulous constipation-easing smoothie on the
next page makes a great breakfast and can help
move things along!

THE REGULAR JOE

5 prunes (stones removed)
5 dates (stones removed)
250ml apple juice
250ml milk, or dairy-free alternative
280g natural yoghurt, or dairy-free alternative
½ tsp cinnamon
a pinch of nutmeg

1. Add all of the ingredients to a blender and whizz until smooth, adding more liquid if it's too thick.

2. Add a couple of ice cubes if you like it chilled, but remember that delicate digestive systems prefer warm food/liquids so you could even warm it up a little.

NOURISHING YOURSELF

We can get so caught up in making sure
that the kids are fed and watered that
we forget ourselves and all too often
reach for caffeine and biscuits to keep
us going. We all love a cuppa and a digestive,
but we need to make sure that we are fuelling
ourselves properly so that we can keep up
with the demands of our littles. See it like
a nourishment food chain — if we aren't full,
we'll have nothing to give.

PREPARATION IS KEY!

We have to be realistic and admit that some
days we are rushing around from here to there
and need to just reach into the fridge and
inhale something on the go. So try to prepare
for that! The night before, chop up lots of veg
and leave it in an airtight container next to
a pot of hummus and then you have a very quick,
but nutritious grab-and-go lunch. Chuck some
eggs on to boil the night before and leave
them in the fridge too. You can't beat a hard-
boiled egg — they keep you full for longer and
are a great protein hit, which is essential
for repairing muscle and keeping your energy
levels up.

REST (AND, IF YOU CAN, SLEEP!)

We seem to have a very stoic response to lack of sleep in our culture — how many times has somebody cracked the joke, 'say goodbye to your sleep!' upon your pregnancy or birth announcement? The reality is, lack of sleep is totally unsustainable and can affect our mental and physical well-being. What we should be focusing on is encouraging families to really prioritise sleep and rest, and sharing ways in which to grab some downtime at every opportunity.

We know that 'sleep when baby sleeps' can be a really annoying phrase, especially if you have other children around, but it really is so important to try to rest during any quiet moments you have. If you can't sleep (sometimes our adrenaline is too high), then just lying down and listening to some calming music will have the same restful effect on the body — don't get too hung up on the sleep part, we just want you to rest.

GET SOME HELP

If you've had a really bad night and you literally can't see how you'll make it through the day, ask a friend or family member to pop

over and hold the baby while you get your
head down for a couple of hours — they will
love being asked and having a chance to
snuggle the baby.

TRY TAG-TEAM SLEEPING

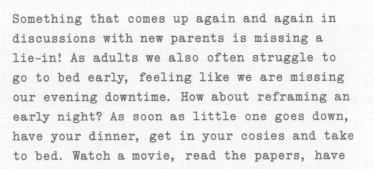

Scheduling in times when you can hand baby
over to your partner for the first half of the
night and go and have a solid uninterrupted
'off duty' sleep is the best tonic. When we
know that we are not 'on call' for baby, we can
often drift into a much deeper sleep, which is
way more restorative than the type you get when
your ears are on stalks. They can then come
and hand baby over to you and take the second
half of the night in a separate room or on the
sofa for their 'off duty' sleep.

HAVE AN EVENING LIE-IN

Something that comes up again and again in
discussions with new parents is missing a
lie-in! As adults we also often struggle to
go to bed early, feeling like we are missing
our evening downtime. How about reframing an
early night? As soon as little one goes down,
have your dinner, get in your cosies and take
to bed. Watch a movie, read the papers, have

a warm drink (caffeine-free) and treat it like your morning lie-in. Because your mind will be relaxing and registering that you are in bed, you're more likely to fall asleep quicker than you ordinarily would too! Double win!

BUILD YOUR TRIBE

If there's one thing we know for certain, it's that we were never meant to parent in isolation. We need people around to help, to lean on and to share tips, advice and stories and have a laugh with. The saying, 'it takes a village to raise a child' is true. If you don't live in one, and especially if you are a single parent, then you can create your tribe in other ways:

- Join groups: NCT, playgroup, baby massage… you name it, they'll be full of other mums needing a tribe just like you.

- Ask a friend or family member with time to come and help you one day a week. Having a set day where you know you'll have back-up can be great for the mind and body.

- Put out an ad or post on social media asking if any other mums locally want to do a regular hang out — you'll be amazed how many other mums out there are just waiting for the offer.

- <u>Swap childcare:</u> if you have a mum friend
  with a baby the same age, do some childcare
  swaps. Watch each other's baby one morning
  a week and gift each other a few hours off.

FRIENDS

Our friendships change throughout the
postnatal period, just as much as we do. You
will meet many new mum friends along the way
who will become your day-to-day support team,
but you will also want to foster friendships
with your 'before kids' friends. One of
the things that can be upsetting is friends
assuming you won't be able to make it to
an event and so not inviting you. Make it
known to your pals that, even though you
may say 'no' a lot, the invites mean a lot
and to keep them coming.

Until you are ready and able to go out for
the evening (tiredness and feeding duties
can definitely stop play in this area), have
a regular evening a month where your close
friends come over for a takeaway and a bottle
of wine. Stay in your PJs (unless you fancy
dressing up) and enjoy catching up, with the
proviso that you may need to be in bed by
10pm! Keeping your friends part of your journey
will allow them to support you better, and

if they also have children, they'll be glad
of the early night.

DON'T FORGET THE OLD YOU

<u>Carving some essential time out, where the
old you can spread your wings or at least
give them a little stretch, is so important.</u>
Many new mums struggle with the huge identity
change and repetitive day-to-day routine when
they become a mum. Yes, they are proud of
this new life role and of their beautiful babe,
but they also wonder where that leaves them,
their passions and their friendships outside
of motherhood.

Sometimes it's while we are away from our
little ones that we can remind ourselves of our
other talents. Plan to do something that makes
you happy; literally WHATEVER floats your boat!
It gives you a little something to look forward
to on the days that can feel a bit repetitive
and challenging. This can often leave you
feeling re-energised and excited to see your
little one again.

SELF-CARE FOR YOUR RELATIONSHIP

Adapting to being parents can put a strain on our relationships, so it's important to carve out a little self-care for these too. When you are both tired and overwhelmed it is easy to take it out on each other and get caught in the resentment rut, or the 'who's more tired' competition.

Here are our tips for keeping on track together:

- Keep talking: this is new for you both and you will both no doubt be managing your feelings in different ways. Keep communicating and asking for help when you need it.

- Do have a date night: it doesn't have to be out. Order in takeaway, light the candles and have a catch up.

- Send each other flirty texts.

- Keep touching: skin-to-skin isn't just for babies. We might not feel like jumping back in the sack just yet, but lying together skin-to-skin, giving each other a little massage or just snuggling up on the sofa, will keep that physical connection ticking over.

You won't always feel like it, but prioritising time for the two of you will help to keep you connected as a team and not bickering with each other — and before long you'll be looking back with hindsight having a chuckle at the expense of the frazzled new parent versions of yourselves.

GETTING BACK IN THE SACK

When you do feel like jumping back in the sack, just remember it may all feel a little different down there (even after a C-section). Hormonal changes can make us a little dry, and so you may benefit from a good organic lube to help you on your way. Take it slow and, remember, if you're not ready, you can have plenty of fun without the penetration.

KEEP RAISING THOSE ENDORPHINS

Endorphins are our feel-good chemicals and, some days, when it all feels too much, we just need to give our endorphins a good kick up the backside. Here are some instant mood lifts:

- Breathe: stop what you are doing and breathe. Inhale through the nose and then slowly breathe out through the mouth, making sure that your out breath is longer than the in breath.

- <u>Drink more water:</u> dehydration can make us feel sluggish and meh!

- <u>Use aromatherapy:</u> add some essential oils to a diffuser, two to three drops to a tissue or a drop on your hand (rub together) and inhale. Lavender, geranium, sweet orange and lemon are all great pick-you-up pongs!

- <u>Move:</u> go for a walk, a run or have a kitchen dance. Just move that body and get the circulation flowing.

- <u>Have a change of scene:</u> change rooms, change house or get outside in the fresh air — as the saying goes, a change is as good as a rest.

REMEMBER, THERE IS NO RIGHT WAY

Forget the one-upmumship. There is no right or wrong way to parent your baby, only the way that works best for you. <u>Even if you are a first-time mum, you will be the expert of your own baby, and your baby will be your best teacher.</u> This is not a competition and therefore you cannot lose; you and your baby will find your own way of doing things and at a pace that is right for you.

...and don't forget – you've got this Mama!

It feels like Jade and I have been talking about having another baby pretty much since Tate arrived.

I think my natural resting state is broody. My ovaries still skip when I think about how it would feel to make another special person to join our family.

And the truth is, at the start of 2020, I was well on my way to going for it. Working so closely with new mums and their babies at Kit & Kin, I had immersed myself in the baby world again and I was nearly ready to take the plunge and start trying for a third. We even got out the box of old babygrows we had put away, to see which ones we could reuse (and realised quite a few of them still had big stains on them! Me and my obsession with white babygrows!).

But then COVID-19 happened, and everything we had taken for granted in life suddenly seemed so fragile. It wasn't only feeling worried about the virus and the impact it might have on us and all our loved ones, although of course that was a concern. It was more this sense of uncertainty, that I know so many of us have felt. Whereas it seemed like I could really do something to help fight climate change, both via Kit & Kin and our own personal efforts as a family, I felt powerless in the face of COVID-19, and the thought of having another child seemed suddenly much less straightforward.

Like a lot of families, we spent many hours at home with our children during the national lockdowns. And despite feeling trapped and missing all our friends and family, we also grew closer and stronger than ever. With only the four of us for company, and none of us rushing around to school or clubs or work, I was so much more present. I really began to appreciate everything we have – we all did; cooking together, playing games, walking our lovely old dog, Jojo.

One thing we all enjoy doing is watching Disney movies (we love a bit of Disney!) and, occasionally, if I planned it right and had enough popcorn at the ready to bribe them with, we'd add a little nature documentary on to the end of the movie, just to make sure we were providing balanced viewing! During the second lockdown of 2020 we watched Sir David Attenborough's *A Life on Our Planet*. The message of his film is simple: we all need to work with nature, not against it; everything we do as individuals has an impact.

One thing that even just considering having another child has made me do is really think about what, if anything, I would do differently this time. What lessons has the older, wiser mum of Beau and Tate got to teach herself, should a new sibling for them ever arrive? There are plenty of little things: guests can wait, sleep when they sleep, give washable nappies a go. Pretty much everything that all the brilliant experts in this book have told you! But I think the one thing I would like to tell myself is to slow down. Slow down, mama.

I was always in such a rush – to get back in shape, to get back to work, to get to the next stage, to get here and get there. I would like to tell that me that there is no rush! These things can wait, stop and enjoy your baby, enjoy the time you have with them. Because it is, of course, such a cliché, but time really does go by so fast. I sit and look at Beau, a teenager, and Tate, about to start senior school, and I really do not know where the years have gone. What wouldn't I give to be able to go back and smell their sweet baby smell? Or run my finger down their little noses and make them giggle, the way they both loved so much? Now all I get is them laughing at my 'mum dancing' as I try to get with the latest TikTok routine.

The other thing I'd like to tell myself is that I know so much more than I think I do. I was such a nervous wreck at times, worrying about doing it 'right', being a good mum, being seen to be a good mum. I didn't realise just how much I already knew, how much of being a mama is instinctive. It's already there. This is what we came to do, mamas!

So try, if you can, to trust yourself and know that you are enough. All your baby really needs is you and, yes mama, you've totally got this!

Signing off, for now.

love, Emma x

Index

Useful Resources

www.nct.org.uk

www.nhs.uk

www.wen.org.uk

www.forestryengland.uk

www.Walkit.com

www.Walkengland.org.uk

www.Walkswithbuggies.com

www.mind.org.uk

FeedFinder - app

Acknowledgements

To my publisher Laura Higginson, thank you for believing in my passion for this book. To Sam Crisp and Sarah Thompson, for listening to me for hours on end talking about my beautiful journey with my babies. To the whole team at Ebury, thank you for helping me bring this book to life. It is my very first book and you made it so much fun to create.

A huge thank you to all the brilliant experts in this book, I wish you all lived with me during my first few years of parenthood!!!

A special spicy thank you to my team Severine Berman, Sophie Renwick, Mark Ashelford, Stuart Freeman, Simon Jones and PJ Bunton, you all know me so well, too well sometimes. You're the best!!!

Ray Burmiston, Lisa Laudat and David Lopez for bringing my cover shoot vision to life and making it a very special day.

Christopher Money, Eve, Jess and our brilliant team at Kit & Kin (so proud) let's keep making this world a better place. We've got this!

My beautiful friends, old, new, mummies and to the original Girl Power crew the Spice Girls! You were all so invaluable in the early years and even more so now. Here's to all my women out there.

My family...I love you. Mum, thank you for always being right by my side. The thing you taught me the most is that I am loved. Jade, my soul mate and my rock. We have been the dream team and you truly are the best partner and daddy in the whole world. I feel so lucky to have you.

Beau and Tate, I cry (happy tears) every time I think of all our beautiful memories. You are my world, my everything, my sunshine. I know I'm always telling you that I LOVE YOU but it's a constant reminder that you are the best thing that ever happened to me. X

Notes

I've left some space for you to jot down your thoughts, feelings and memories of your first year of being a mama.

Mama You Got This

Mama You Got This

Ebury Press, an imprint of Ebury Publishing.
20 Vauxhall Bridge Road, London SW1V 2SA

Ebury Press is part of the Penguin Random
House group of companies whose addresses can
be found at global.penguinrandomhouse.com

Penguin
Random House
UK

First published by Ebury Press in 2021
www.penguin.co.uk

A CIP catalogue record for this book
is available from the British Library

ISBN 9781529104561

Project Editor: Sam Crisp
Text Design: Studio Polka
Photography: Ray Burmiston Cover
and p2
Getty p32, 37, 47, 71, 93, 103, 133,
and 185
Mark Hayman p145, 147, and 181
Emma Tunbridge p149 and 175
Illustrations: May van Millingen

Colour origination: Altaimage London
Printed and bound in Italy by Printer Trento

The authorised representative in the EEA is Penguin
Random House Ireland, Morrison Chambers, 32
Nassau Street, Dublin D02 YH68.

Penguin Random House is committed to a
sustainable future for our business, our readers
and our planet. This book is made from Forest
Stewardship Council® certified paper.